STRATAGEM

ABOUT THE AUTHOR

JOHN MUCAI HOLDS A PH.D. in Business Administration from the University of Nairobi. He is a Certified Public Accountant of Kenya too. He is an alumnus of United States International University, where he graduated with an MSc in Management and Organizational Development and cum laude in BSc in Information Systems & Technology. He retired from Coca-Cola East & Central Africa Ltd in 2017 and has since been pursuing various hobbies and entrepreneurial interests.

STRATAGEM

Developing a Strategic Mindset

John Mucai

"The essence of strategy is choosing what not to do."

—MICHAEL PORTER

To my wife, Susan, my son Allan, and my daughter Anne, who are the primary source of inspiration and encouragement for the MUCAI Quick Read series.

CONTENTS

LIST OF TABLES

LIST OF FIGURES

FOREWORD

Behind every story of success is strategy. But what is a good strategy, one might ask? The author suggests that a good strategy is difficult to describe but is easy to recognize, just like beauty.

Numerous books exist on different aspects of strategy. It may sometimes be challenging for a newcomer to discover its true essence without spending many hours poring through the literature and seeing strategy presented from multiple angles. Such an exercise may often result in feelings of discontentment. Yet strategy is such an important discipline in many areas of life. The author of Stratagem is a strategy practitioner and recognizes this shortcoming.

Stratagem approaches strategy from an angle that will appeal to any reader, whether or not they have encountered the subject before. The book gives a fresh lease of life to a subject that may seem ridden with choking obfuscation.

John Mucai

Hopefully, the book will spark an interest in strategy. If this happens, one of the key objectives of the MUCAI Quick Read series will have been accomplished. Please visit _mucaiquickread.com_ for more information on the series.

PREFACE

During the last ten years of my career in the corporate world, I spent much time with many talented colleagues developing corporate, business, and functional strategies. Those with degrees from business schools had the edge over others. But the reality was that many talented individuals who rose to senior management functional positions had not undergone formal strategy training. Yet, they were expected to participate effectively in the strategy-making process.

During all that time, I was struck by the range of approaches used in the strategy-making process. In almost all instances, the finished product was impressive - perhaps a tribute to the high quality of the talent in the organization. But that notwithstanding, I always harbored a nudging desire to write a book articulating the true essence of strategy in a straightforward fashion. A book that would help managers and others in leadership positions gain confidence in developing strategies for their respective areas of jurisdiction. I hope this book will fulfill that purpose.

In keeping with the MUCAI Quick Read series' philosophy, I have avoided presenting the material in a textbook format and tended towards a storytelling bias.

I have included tables and figures in the few instances where I strongly feel a narrative would be insufficient. As the saying goes, "A picture speaks louder than a thousand words." Hopefully, the tables and figures will enhance the understanding of those who are new to the strategy-making process

I know that I would be speaking on behalf of all strategy practitioners if I said that the project called "life" is primarily strategy-driven. Accordingly, one of my aims in the book is to demonstrate this point using stories. But I must hasten to point out that the stories of Sukuma Wiki and Akili Mali narrated in the book are fictional.

ACKNOWLEDGMENTS

The Almighty God has been the shining guiding light throughout my life, even in this book project. I will always remain steadfastly thankful to Him.

This book would not have been possible without the ongoing unshakeable support of my wife, Susan, my son Allan, and my daughter Anne. I am deeply grateful to them.

I would also like to thank Teddy Muhia and Nzisa Kattambo for reviewing the book and offering invaluable feedback.

PART I

THE CONTEXT OF STRATEGY

CHAPTER 1

Introduction

*"It's okay to get lost every once in a while,
sometimes getting lost is how we find ourselves."*
—Robert Tew

I CANNOT REMEMBER HOW I behaved when I was a toddler. But by observing toddlers' behavior today, I can confidently say that our lives are driven by strategy from the time we set foot on this earth. Let us consider one example.

Crying is one of the most effective strategies babies use when they feel hungry. They know intuitively that the louder they cry, the quicker the mother will bring milk to them. This strategy works almost all the time, and babies know it.

It does not stop at that. Babies have other hardwired strategies for dealing with unpleasant strangers. In military parlance, those strategies may collectively be called "shock and awe."

The strategies are common among the infant community and will be left to the reader's imagination.

As the baby grows older and starts making a few steps, they scan the external environment. Through subtle toddler analysis, the baby makes strategic choices on the actions that will optimize the quest for happiness. This includes touching and playing with anything that looks interesting. It also includes mixing and mashing anything and everything to see the outcome. Some babies are also keen on identifying barriers, climbing over them, knocking them out of the way, or using other means to overcome them.

What these examples illustrate is that strategic thinking is wired in our DNA.

There is also a moral to this story, namely, that you should not take children for granted. For a newly minted business manager whose responsibility of crafting business strategies has been thrust upon them, the toddler story demonstrates that there is hope.

* * *

In the hectic world of adults, developing organizational strategies can be daunting. Where do you start? How do you do it? And how can you be sure you are doing the right thing to obtain the right results?

The truth is that there is no "silver bullet." There are multiple ways of developing strategies. You can follow certain tried and tested methods to achieve decent outcomes.

The following chapters are intended to assist you in accomplishing these purposes in straightforward ways. This is not intended to be a textbook on strategy. It is a storybook of strategy.

CHAPTER 2

Sukuma Wiki Pet Food Shop

"By three methods we may learn wisdom: First, by reflection, which is noblest; second, by imitation, which is easiest; and third by experience, which is the bitterest."
— *Confucius*

ONCE UPON A TIME IN THE beautiful land of Kenya, there lived an enterprising young gentleman named Sukuma Wiki. He was tall, charming, and blessed with a natural wittiness that endeared him to almost everyone he encountered. It was not a wonder he had risen to several leadership positions in high school, including class prefect when he was in Form 3 and head boy in his final year of high school.

Sukuma Wiki was also one of the most visible individuals in the university's Veterinary School, partly because of his height but mainly because of his verbosity, which had seen him elected leader of the university students' union. He graduated from university with a bachelor's degree in veterinary medicine.

Sukuma Wiki did not take long to get a job after graduation. And although his employer had given him much leeway to operate independently, Sukuma Wiki was not content working for somebody else. In his mind, his employment with Sasumua Veterinary Clinic was only temporary. His heart was elsewhere. He yearned to become his own boss.

One day, while on duty at the residence of one of Sasumua Veterinary Clinic's clients, he was accidentally bitten by an aggressive Rottweiler. The dog bit him on his left hand, leaving him with severe bruises that took several days to heal. It was a freak event. He had handled even more vicious dogs previously.

Two months later, Sukuma Wiki was attacked by a Pitt Bull brought by the owner to the clinic. It was not a serious incident. He was not injured.

However, despite his outward confidence, Sukuma Wiki was quite superstitious. On the day he was attacked by the Pitt Bull, he concluded that something about him and dogs did not mix well, which could ultimately lead to an even more unpleasant outcome. He reasoned that the second event was a supernatural subliminal signal that it was time for him to move on.

One month after the second dog attack incident and three years and two months after qualifying as a veterinary doctor, Sukuma Wiki quit his job at Sasumua Veterinary Clinic. He decided to enter the exciting and lucrative world of business.

* * *

Sukuma Wiki had accumulated savings of KShs 3 million. He believed this sum was enough to set him on the right path in business. He only needed an additional KShs 2 million, which he could obtain quickly from one of the local banks. Many of these banks targeted the country's rapidly expanding small and medium-sized enterprises.

Sukuma Wiki loved cats and dogs immensely. He believed that his best bet was to start a business that would allow him to continue caring for pets in new and different ways.

* * *

Five days after leaving Sasumua Veterinary Clinic, several questions started circulating in his mind as he lay on his bed: What have I got myself into? Will my education in veterinary science go to waste? Why do dogs hate me so much? Is it something to do with my height or my voice? What will the friends I left in the dog world say about me? Who will take care of Maskan, my favorite dog? As Sukuma Wiki ruminated over the endless questions, he quietly fell asleep.

As he transitioned from non-sleep to REM sleep, he saw a small, hairy black dog running towards him from a distance. It was a poodle. The poodle was barking and seemed to be in distress.

As the poodle approached him, its characteristics changed. It became a brownish Chihuahua. And as the Chihuahua came closer, he realized it was a Labrador Retriever. But no! It was a German Shepherd. And it was not barking. It was laughing. It was saying in a soft feminine voice, "Sukuma, why are you breathing so heavily, honey?" The German Shepherd, which had by now become a giant of a dog, jumped on him. He shouted, "Ahhhhhhh," and woke up, only to find his wife, Anita, leaning on one of her ankles beside him, staring at him intently.

"Why are you shouting, Sukuma?" Anita asked him.

"Nothing. Just dogs," Sukuma Wiki responded politely, then went back to sleep.

Several hours later, while deep in REM, Sukuma Wiki dreamt that he had become Nairobi's biggest pet food supplier. Anita was his partner. The business had become the envy of all pet food shops in Nairobi. He dreamt of eventually becoming a pet food manufacturer, supplying different types of pet foods to all pet shops in all corners of Kenya.

The vividness of that dream was astonishing. From then on, it became clear to Sukuma Wiki that he was destined to enter the pet foods business.

* * *

One month later, Sukuma Wiki was seated at his desk at home, trying to chart his way forward. The idea of setting out on the journey towards the pet food business was daunting but an exciting prospect.

The next day, he called friends to find out where he could set up shop. It was not as easy as he had assumed. The monthly rental for shop premises ranged from KShs 20,000/= to KShs 100,000/=. He had to start with a low budget, so he opted to rent premises at Kawangware shopping center at a monthly rental of KShs 25,000/=.

The shop was big enough to accommodate ample supplies of different types of pet food. Additionally, there was a backroom that he and Anita could use as an office.

Sukuma Wiki was action-oriented. He did not waste time. He signed the lease contract for the premises and procured stocks to put in the shop. He also called many of his former clients at Sasumua Veterinary Clinic to inform them of his exciting new venture and asked them to contact him for their future supplies of pet foods.

Sukuma Wiki hired Eunice Mrembo, a young high school graduate, as a shop assistant. He also recruited two youngsters from the neighborhood, Martin Sungura and Gideon Mjanja, to work as casual workers. Finally, he invested in a used pick-up truck that he would use to collect supplies from manufacturers and make deliveries to customers.

* * *

Setting up the shop was exciting and fulfilling to Sukuma Wiki and Anita. There was something about it that was difficult to describe.

Sukuma Wiki was elated when the first customer entered the shop to inquire about maize germ for his cows. Although he did not stock the item, it was pleasing to receive the inquiry.

The second customer asked for a dog chain. He did not have it in stock either. Five other customers visited the shop later in the day. Most of the items that they needed were not available. Sukuma Wiki fulfilled the requirements of only one customer. So, it was not an incredibly successful day. Still, Sukuma Wiki and Anita had gained a better understanding of Kawangware customers' needs. Sukuma Wiki and Anita made a note to procure the missing items, granted that the items were not part of the pet food shop's core business.

The traffic in the shop on the second day was a little disappointing. Only two customers entered the shop, and only one of them made a purchase—rat poison. The other customer wandered around the shop without uttering a word and then walked out.

The third day was also not very encouraging, nor were the fourth, fifth, and sixth.

What was going on, Sukuma Wiki wondered? But he was an optimist. He believed strongly that things would turn around in due course. Several years earlier, he had read in a business magazine that new businesses took time before gaining traction. So, there was still some hope.

One bright Saturday morning, Sukuma Wiki got a brilliant idea. It was such a stroke of genius that it almost jolted him out of his seat as he wallowed in the emotion triggered by its innovativeness.

He immediately called one of his former clients, Mr. Eric Wooden. Mr. Wooden was the chairman of the Pets Club of Langata and Karen and owned several dogs himself. Sukuma Wiki was sure that if Mr. Wooden bought supplies from him, it would open the door for other customers who were members of the Pets Club of Langata and Karen.

That was the big breakthrough he had been awaiting for several weeks.

* * *

Mr. Wooden decided to make a surprise visit to Sukuma Wiki's shop. They were good friends, and he wanted to humor Sukuma Wiki.

On the day Mr. Wooden went to the Sukuma Wiki Pet Shop, he experienced something that would go straight into his incomplete memoirs.

He rarely asked anyone for directions; instead, he preferred to follow the directions in Google Maps. On that day, he found himself traversing through a slum area in Kawangware. People looked at him like he was an animal in a zoo.

There was hardly any parking space near Sukuma Wiki's shop, so he was forced to park his vehicle about 100 meters away.

As he alighted from his car, Mr. Wooden said a short prayer. He needed it.

Three street boys followed him slowly, trying to speak to him in English. He reciprocated by trying to talk in broken Kiswahili. It did not work. The boys laughed when he uttered the first few words, creating quite a scene.

One of the boys seemed to want to show off his English language skills to Mr. Wooden and repeatedly said, "Very very good," to which Mr. Wooden responded absent-mindedly, "Yes Yes Yes."

After what seemed like a lifetime, Mr. Wooden eventually arrived at Sukuma Wiki's shop.

He had reasoned that Sukuma Wiki would escort him back to the car, shielding him from the marauding street urchins. But Sukuma Wiki was not in the shop. He had gone to collect supplies of pet food from the industrial area. Mr. Wooden's face turned red as he gradually absorbed the disappointing information.

Mr. Wooden did not even bother to inquire about pet food. His mind was now entirely preoccupied with strategizing how he would make it back to the safety of his car. He quickly left the shop.

He walked in exceptionally long strides, desperate to outpace the street boys who could not leave him to walk in peace.

He pretended to smile as he returned to the vehicle, putting on a brave face in a sea of potential danger. Every human being he met on his way conjured up images of a dangerous criminal.

He vividly remembered a movie he had watched in the comfort of his splendid house at Karen. In the movie, gangs chased a white tourist in dark alleys in a slum area of a big city in Africa. Two policemen eventually saved the tourist and asked for a small payment in return for saving his life and possessions.

But here he was, without even a penny in his pocket and no idea how to contact the police if something nasty happened. He said another short prayer when he found himself 20 meters from his car.

When he finally got inside the car, two long lifetimes had passed since the last time he had been in it, he said another short prayer, this time seeking divine intervention to enable him to exit the slum area and return to his wife, Sharon, in Karen in one whole piece. He prayed for journey mercies.

✳ ✳ ✳

Thirty minutes later, Mr. Wooden was back on the main road. He sighed a sigh of tremendous relief. He could not wait to return to his home in Karen to describe his horrifying experience to Sharon.

He had been to hell and back as far as he could tell.

When he stepped out of his car, the first sentence he uttered summed up the results of his desire to surprise his friend Sukuma Wiki.

"The hooligans even plucked out one of the side mirrors. Damn!"

That would be the last time Mr. Wooden would even contemplate visiting the Sukuma Wiki Pet Food shop or any other shop in its vicinity.

Several weeks later, when he ran into Sukuma Wiki at a mall in Karen, he learned, to his astonishment, that he had taken a wrong turn at Kawangware on his way to the Sukuma Wiki Pet Shop. There was a better and shorter route from the highway.

However, in Mr. Wooden's mind, the damage had already been done. He would never again take such big risks just to please his friend, Sukuma Wiki.

* * *

As days turned into weeks and weeks turned into months, things at the Sukuma Wiki Pet Food Shop at Kawangware worsened.

One sunny Monday morning, as Sukuma Wiki reviewed mail he had retrieved from the post office, he came across a rather nastily worded letter from one of his suppliers.

The supplier threatened to halt further supplies until Sukuma Wiki regularized his account, which was 90 days past due and had an outstanding balance of KShs 200,000/=. The supplier would take legal action if Sukuma Wiki did not settle the outstanding amount within 30 days.

This letter would not have been a significant concern were it not for the fact that the balance in Sukuma Wiki's bank account stood at KShs 50,000/=, and the stock he had bought from the supplier had hardly moved.

After fully absorbing the contents of the letter and weighing up his options, Sukuma Wiki uttered words that were completely uncharacteristic of him: "Who the hell does he think he is? His pet food is crap anyway." He uttered other obscenities, which Eunice Mrembo overheard.

He cursed further for having made a slow-moving purchase and, worst of all, for purchasing the pet food from such a callous supplier.

He could not return the items to the supplier. The best he could do was plead with the supplier for more time to repay the debt. But how could he even master the courage to talk to the supplier? This was too much!

Anita had not joined him in the shop on that day, so he did not have anyone to vent his frustrations to.

And as if the overdue debt for dog meal supplies was not annoying enough, Sukuma Wiki received an unexpected visit from the Kenya Revenue Authority officers as he was about to close the shop. He had not filed his VAT returns and was behind in VAT remittances. The delays had attracted interest and penalties. There was no room for negotiation. This particular visit was exceptionally infuriating.

It was as if the Langata Rottweiller and the Sasumua Pit Bull had mutated into dog meal suppliers and government tax collectors! Indeed, as one of the tax collectors spoke angrily, Sukuma Wiki could not help noticing his sharp, almost dog-like canines.

* * *

When he returned home later in the early evening, Sukuma Wiki was fuming like a hungry lion that had just missed catching its prey.

As he walked into the living room, everything within two feet of his feet was in danger.

He angrily kicked a stool. The stool rolled across the room until it came to rest after knocking another taller stool. There was a flower vase on the second stool. The vase wiggled on its base for two seconds, then fell to the floor, exploding like a mini-grenade, breaking into pieces, and gushing out water in multiple directions. A few droplets splashed on Anita's kitten, Kapusy, who was sleeping on the carpet near a window. The kitten sprinted across the room and jumped onto one of the window ledges, screaming, "miaou miaaaau."

The strange commission in the living room disrupted Anita, who was cutting up cabbage in the kitchen. She rushed out to find out what was happening. As she entered the living room, she found Sukuma Wiki talking to himself.

"Who do they think they are?" Sukuma Wiki shouted in a rage as if addressing Anita.

"What are you talking about, Sukuma?" she asked.

"And please calm down. You are not yourself, Sukuma. What is going on?" she added.

"Can you believe that the tax folks are demanding KShs 500,000/=, most of which is penalties? I thought the government was supposed to assist small business people like us, not destroy us," Sukuma Wiki said.

* * *

The conversation with Anita continued for another hour before Sukuma Wiki could calm down. But his last few words seemed to have unleashed another unexpected storm.

"And why are you looking at me like that anyway? You are the one who convinced me that traders at Kawangware did not bother remitting VAT to the KRA. Now see what has happened!" Sukuma Wiki said.

Anita could not take the attack on her character. She ran into the bedroom sobbing and banged the door behind her. She knelt beside the bed and placed her cute face in her soft palms. She continued sobbing in low tones, occasionally crying in fits and starts. This emotional outburst continued for ten minutes.

It was too much for her. How could Sukuma Wiki make such accusations against her?

Then, the thought came rushing into her mind like a bullet. During a visit to Sukuma Wiki's parents eight months earlier, Sukuma Wiki's mother had asked her to exercise utmost patience, even during times of hardship, just as she had vowed when getting married to Sukuma Wiki. But the point that had stuck in Anita's mind as if glued there with chewing gum was what Sukuma Wiki's mother had said should happen if things got out of hand, namely, that Anita should never hesitate to call her anytime for motherly advice. That memory triggered Anita into action.

Anita placed the call to Sukuma Wiki's mother. Sukuma Wiki's mother responded after only two rings.

"Hello, Anita!"

"Hello, mum!"

"Are you crying, my daughter? What is wrong, honey?

"Sukuma Wiki has become a monster, mum!"

"A monster? What is going on, dear?"

"A short while ago, he attacked Kapusy without any provocation whatsoever. The cat ran out of the house, meowing. It has probably been knocked down by a car by now. Now, I do not know what to do."

"Stop crying, darling. The cat will be fine."

"He also accused me of colluding with Kawangware traders to cause trouble for him with KRA."

"How can he do that? Is Sukuma there?"

"Yes."

"I will call him right now," Sukuma's mother said and hung up.

Sukuma Wiki was not in the mood for phone calls, but he could not ignore his mother's call.

There were no greetings. Sukuma Wiki's mother went straight to the point.

"Sukuma! What have you done to Anita?

"Nothing, mum."

"And why is she so upset?"

"I am a little confused, mum. I have not done anything to upset her."

"But did you attack her cat?"

"Oh, that! I am sorry, mum. I could not help it. I am just having a few problems with the business. I was a bit stressed out and may have frightened the cat. I did not attack it."

"What problems are you having with the shop, son?"

"Business is very slow, mum. And now my biggest supplier is threatening legal action if I do not clear a huge debt. Everything seems to be going bonkers."

"Don't worry, son. There are more important things in life than a pet food shop. If it is giving you such headaches, maybe you should consider returning to your original veterinary doctor career. Think about it, son."

That last sentence was like a breath of fresh air. Somehow, it seemed to calm Sukuma Wiki like a tranquilizer. Why had he not thought about it earlier?

That is why God made "mums," Sukuma Wiki concluded.

* * *

Later that evening, when Anita calmed down, Sukuma Wiki approached her and spoke politely.

"I have had it, Anita. I cannot continue like this. I would rather go back to my profession in veterinary medicine. I will call Jack at Sasumua Clinic tomorrow morning to ask whether they can take me back. I was quite happy working there were it not for the two incidents with the two crazy dogs. Damn, the world of the pet food business!"

* * *

During the next month, Sukuma Wiki spent most of his time looking for someone to buy the business. He was careful not to betray his desperation to potential buyers. He told them that he had decided to go back into the profession to continue pursuing what he believed was ground-breaking research on comparative animal psychology - a project that would require 100% of his attention without the distractions of the pet food shop.

He sold the business to Akili Mali, a University of Nairobi School of Business graduate whose late uncle had bequeathed him KShs 3 million.

* * *

On the day Sukuma Wiki signed the contract to sell the pet foods business and received the KShs 2 million from Akili Mali, he took Anita for dinner at one of the top-end restaurants in Nairobi. The dinner was to celebrate the end of a near-financial catastrophe.

For the starter, Anita ordered delicious grilled scallops with n'duja butter. Sukuma Wiki went for moules marinière, a tasty serving of mussels in white wine sauce.

Sukuma Wiki asked Anita to be bold in her thinking as she selected the main course. He reminded her that were it not for the good angels in heaven, even the money for dinner would have evaporated into thin air several days earlier.

Accordingly, Anita ordered roast duck breast with figs, rosemary, and garlic fried potatoes. She did not bother to check the price on the menu.

Sukuma Wiki did not exercise any restraint, either. He ordered roasted skate wings and charred baby leeks served with a creamy, buttery sauce. He also ordered a selection of tropical vegetables, steamed to the utmost delight by the One-Star Michelin chef.

However, the quantities on the plates were relatively small. Sukuma Wiki and especially Anita were used to large portions, and this celebratory day would not end in disappointment. Accordingly, Sukuma Wiki ordered an additional meal, an exquisite Turkey Piccata with jacketed potatoes, which he shared with Anita.

The couple indulged in 1948 Beeslaar Pinotage Stellenbosch wine, too.

For dessert, Sukuma Wiki chose warm sponge pudding. Anita, who had a sweet tooth, chose deep-fried sweets called Gulab Jamun.

After sharing stories of their time at the Kawangare pet food shop and almost laughing their lungs out, Sukuma Wiki and Anita danced for about 30 minutes, then left for home feeling completely elated.

Before falling asleep, Sukuma Wiki's last words were a fitting conclusion to an extraordinary life event earlier that evening. He simply said: "Life is wonderful," and collapsed into a pleasant slumber.

* * *

The following morning, when Sukuma Wiki woke up, he sat on the side of his bed. As he looked for his slippers to walk to the bathroom to shower, he decided to peruse the papers on top of his bedside table.

One thing that stood out was a long, two-inch wide piece of paper the waiter had handed him the previous night after running the credit card. When he looked at it, he quickly returned to the warm blankets.

He wanted to forget the figure he had seen at the bottom of the slip as quickly as possible. There was also a hand-written number with the word "Tip" in front of it and a large circle around it, which had caused him some nausea and an olfactory hallucination.

He wished that when he eventually woke up later in the day, he would discover that the preceding 20 hours were all part of a bold bad dream. But that was not to be. The results of doing "life" without well-thought-out strategies were real!

PART II

BACKGROUND OF STRATEGY

CHAPTER 3

What is Strategy?

"The essence of strategy is choosing what not to do."
—Michael Porter

THE VERY FIRST PROBLEM THAT newcomers to strategy run into is the multiplicity of definitions and descriptions of strategy. The volume of literature on this topic is mind-boggling.

Simply put, a strategy is a well-thought-out means to a desired end. As simple as that.

If, after reading this sentence, you put away this book and go off on other pursuits, you can do so knowing, without any shadow of a doubt, that you know the meaning of strategy.

* * *

But we need to unpack this definition of strategy a little more to expose its simplicity fully.

Let us suppose you are a pygmy who lives in the thick Congo forest. You have stayed for two weeks without consuming any animal protein, and your body is beginning to ask for replenishment. You decide to do something to solve the problem.

What would you do if you were the pygmy? An excellent solution would be to develop and deploy a strategy as efficiently as possible.

You would not need PowerPoint to articulate the strategy. If you did, you would probably starve to death or develop a severe protein deficiency. But you are a pygmy and cannot let such technological barriers get in your way.

One strategy would be to reach out to your fellow pygmies to form a hunting team. The team would then determine which part of the forest would be ideal for game hunting. If there were other forest dwellers, the chances are that those other forest dwellers would be involved in hunting, too. Therefore, your team would have to consider how best to outdo the other forest dwellers. The team would also identify the specific animal they would hunt and the types of weapons they would use.

The scenario would be significantly more complicated if you lived in a forest with multiple villages. You would have to consider how people in other villages would respond to your hunting enterprise. If they felt threatened that you were interfering with the source of their livelihood, you would have to consider whether to direct your hunting efforts to another location.

Alternatively, you could consider collaborating with people from other villages to increase manpower for the hunt, ensure success in game hunting, and share the bounty.

Other considerations would be the competence of the individuals in the hunting team, the allocation of the hunting tools, and the coordination of the hunting mission.

So, as you can see, the simple decision to change your diet for the week could quickly mutate into a significant undertaking involving multiple people and assets.

The degree of elaborateness in the approach that you and your team would use to hunt for the animal would vary depending on multiple factors: the abundance of game in the forest, the type of game, the tools available for hunting, the composition of the hunting team, and other factors.

The means you would deploy to hunt for the game is called strategy.

The effectiveness of the strategy would invariably be proportional to thoughtfulness in preparation.

If you simply rushed into the forest with a spear, looking for an animal to kill, the chances are that you would not achieve much. You could potentially even end up inside the stomach of a wild animal.

The amazing thing is that strategy is essential and can be extremely complicated, even for something as simple as hunting.

* * *

It is not easy to think of any endeavor in life where a certain level of strategy is not required. If one wishes to achieve something, one must have a strategy to help him achieve it. Strategy is essential in the military, business, and other aspects of life. By doing it deliberately and methodically, one Is likely to accomplish their purposes efficiently and effectively.

A Tale of Strategy in the Village

Where I come from, there is a story that children are told by their mothers, aunties, or grandmas to illustrate the community's distaste for bad manners. Professors of business schools would probably enjoy listening to this story as it goes deeply into certain aspects of strategy. It goes like this:

Part 1

Many years ago, there was a character called Njoroge who was very lazy. He did not have a wife to cook for him, nor did he try to cook for himself, so he deployed a brilliant survival strategy.

Around lunchtime, he would walk around the village, paying attention to identify a home where dishes were being prepared to serve lunch. If he sensed that a meal was about to be served, he would walk in uninvited precisely when the meal was being served. Talk of strategy!

Given the community's culture of generosity, the lady of the house would invite Njoroge to partake in the meal. Of course, Njoroge would pretend that his visit at mealtime was purely coincidental. Talk of tactics!

Part 2

Although the village was extensive, Njoroge's strategy was not sustainable in the long run. His timing did not work well on several occasions, and he would miss out on the meal. But Njoroge was a master of strategy.

One memorable day, he entered a home just in the nick of time. The lady of the house was putting food on the last few plates. On noticing the risk of missing out yet again on partaking in the meal, Njoroge quickly said: "Nyina wa Kamau, ndukanjikirire nyingi. Reke njiganie icio." [Mother of Kamau, that portion you have on the plate right now is enough for me, thank you.] The lady of the house was too embarrassed not to give the food to Njoroge.

Many people narrated this story in jest and typically followed it with a speech on the community's abhorrence of the type of conduct demonstrated by Njoroge.

As Porter (2015) would say: "The sign of a good strategy is that it makes some customers unhappy."[1] Njoroge's obnoxious strategies annoyed some of the fictional village's ladies.[2]

CHAPTER 4

Strategy in the Military

"The supreme art of war is to subdue the enemy without fighting."
—Sun Tzu

THE WORD STRATEGY COMES FROM the Greek word "strategos." Strategos refers to the art of the general. The "activity" strategy was there even before the invention of the word strategy in the late Eighteenth Century (early 19th Century). Embedded in the idea of strategy is the desire to have better control of the future.

For centuries, military thought centered around clashes between cultural heroes and emperors. Combat was part of the historical evolution of states. For example, the ancient history of China is replete with accounts of warfare.

People have historically jostled for power in different ways, giving rise to ever-increasing development and refinement of instruments of warfare.

Over time, the need for studying battlefield lessons increased. People were intent on preserving the tactics that worked and discarding the mistakes that occurred during battles.

Many of the works memorializing warfare in China were lost for various reasons. Sun Tzu's "Art of War" is one of the few valuable remaining works. The work has been influential in the military and other areas such as business and personal life.[3]

Sun Tzu's Biography

There is scant information about Sun Tzu's biography. Some historians even debate whether a person named Sun Tzu existed. However, the recent discovery of ancient "Art of War" manuscripts suggests he existed.[4]

The historical record suggests that he was born around 500 BCE in the Chinese state of Ch'i during the Chou dynasty. He joined the army there and later became an army strategist and general.[5]

Sun Tzu wrote The Art of War around 481-221 BCE when the Chinese states were engaged in incessant warfare as they sought control of China. At that time, the conduct of war followed traditions and protocols. Hardly any state had an advantage over another. The tactics on the battlefield were predictable. The wars were "boring" and yielded minimum results for the warring parties, leading to frustration.

Sun Tzu saw things differently. He believed that winning a war required more than chivalry on the battlefield. It required strategic maneuvering to leverage one's strengths and capitalize on the enemy's weaknesses.

By deploying the strategies described by Sun Tzu, particularly the principle of total war, Ying Sheng, the King of Qin, conquered the other states in China in quick succession: Han in 230 BCE; Wei five years later in 225 BCE; Chu three years later in 223 BCE; Zhao and Yan one year later in 222; and, finally, Qi in 221 BCE. See Figure 1.

Ying Sheng then established the Qin dynasty (221–206 BCE) and declared himself the first emperor of China.[6]

Figure 1: The states of China c. 260 BCE

The war that led to the creation of the unified Chinese state under Ying Sheng's rule must be one of the most exciting stories in military strategy.

Sun Tzu's writings have been studied and successfully deployed by military generals for generations. At some point, the strategic principles outlined in "The Art of War" became the *modus operandi* in the military and were also used by business leaders to achieve business goals.[7]

Snapshot of "The Art of War"

"The Art of War" is divided into 13 chapters, each covering a particular military strategy. It is fascinating reading for anyone interested in studying strategy.[8]

The first paragraph of the first chapter provides a good glimpse of what to expect in the book:

Warfare is the greatest affair of state, the basis of life and death, the Way (Tao) to survival or extinction. It must be thoroughly pondered and analyzed.

Sun Tzu then lays out the need for careful, methodical planning before engaging in warfare to ensure success with minimal loss of life and property on either side of a conflict.

A unique characteristic of "The Art of War" is its conciseness. It is overwhelming in its compactness.

The key ideas fall under eight headings: general principles, the commander's qualifications, strategy, and tactics; deception and formless; configurations of terrain; spirit and command; strategic configuration of power; and the orthodox and unorthodox.[9]

＊ ＊ ＊

The **general principles** include developing a strategy to ensure that the populace will provide total allegiance to the ruler; the primary objective of war is subjugating the enemy without necessarily engaging in combat; maintaining self-control at all times; striving to do things based on objective reasoning; and, carrying out detailed analysis based on concrete data before undertaking a military campaign.

The analysis should be 360 degrees, namely, analysis of the enemy, your forces, and the terrain where the military engagement will occur.

Sun Tzu provides paired criteria that a commander should use to guide the analysis: heaven vs. earth; offense vs. defense; advance vs. retreat; unorthodox vs. orthodox; hunger vs. satiety; exhaustion vs. rest; order vs. disorder; fear vs. confidence; cold vs. warm, and laxity vs. alertness.

Accordingly, the commander should deploy military tactics that are comparatively advantageous vis-a-vis the enemy. For example, if the enemy is exhausted, that would be the right time to attack them. Conversely, the commander should not commit his troops if they are hungry.

Subjective emotions such as fear, anger, and hatred should never be allowed to cloud decision-making. This could result in troops committing to battle unnecessarily, with the attendant risk of losing the battle. Decisions should always be based on an objective evaluation of the situation. Generally, engaging in warfare does not make sense if the state is not in danger. Similarly, if a commander determines that his army is at a disadvantage, he should exercise restraint and not engage in warfare. This is not cowardice but wisdom. To quote Sun Tzu:

If it is not advantageous, do not move. If objectives cannot be attained, do not employ the army. Unless endangered do not engage in warfare. The ruler cannot mobilize the army out of personal anger. The general can not engage in battle because of personal frustration. When it is advantageous, move; when not advantageous, stop. Anger can revert to happiness, annoyance can revert to joy, but a vanquished state cannot be revived, the dead cannot be brought to life. [10]

Sun Tzu provides two perspectives regarding the **commander's qualifications**.

Firstly, he calls out the strengths of a good commander and the corresponding weaknesses. A good commander should have wisdom, knowledge, and credibility. He should be strict, benevolent, and courageous.

Further, a good commander should be a skillful analyst and be unconcerned with fame. Equally, he should be unconcerned with punishment, place the army first, be tranquil, obscure, upright, self-disciplined, strong, clever, inventive, and possess holistic talents.

Weaknesses to look for are being unenlightened, brutalizing and fearing the masses, not being strict, loving the people, being committed to life, being obsessed with fame, being easily angered, hasty, and weak.

The second perspective offered by Sun Tzu is that the astute general looks for these character traits in the enemy and exploits them to his advantage.

In terms of **strategy and tactics**, Sun Tzu avers that the grand strategy is the manipulation of the enemy, creating an opportunity for victory and applying the maximum pressure at the right time. The tactics to achieve this may include luring the enemy to a battle terrain where they would be significantly disadvantaged, using speed and surprise to attack the enemy, and avoiding a strong force when it makes sense. Sun Tzu says:

One who knows the enemy and knows himself will not be endangered in a hundred engagements. One who does not know the enemy but knows himself will sometimes be victorious, sometimes meet with defeat. One who knows neither the enemy nor himself will invariably be defeated in every engagement.

In other words, one must know the enemy. And this will require gathering the necessary intelligence using spies.

Regarding **deception and formless**, the words of Sun Tzu speak for themselves:

Warfare is the Way (Tao) of deception. Thus although [you are] capable, display incapability to them. When committed to employing your forces, feign inactivity. When [your objective] is nearby, make it appear as if distant; when far away, create the illusion of being nearby.

In other words, confuse the enemy so that he responds the way you want, then exploit the situation.

Sun Tsu states that warfare is about deception, false appearances, spreading misinformation, trickery, and deceit. However, the secrecy of one's capabilities is of the utmost importance.

Turning to **configurations and terrain**, Sun Tzu describes the different types of terrain and successfully maneuvering one's forces through the terrain during combat.

In terms of **spirit and command**, Sun Tzu emphasizes that troops must be well-trained, well-fed, and well-equipped so that they can engage in battle with high morale and vigor. A general must think of the converse regarding the enemy – for example, attacking the enemy when the soldiers' morale is low or when they are tired and returning to the camp.

Regarding the **strategic configuration of power**, Sun Tzu is referring to a strategic position that provides the commander with maximum potential power:

One who employs strategic power commands men in battle as if he were rolling logs and stones. The nature of wood and stone is to be quiet when stable but to move when on precipitous ground. If they are square they stop, if round they tend to move. Thus the strategic power of one who excels at employing men in warfare is comparable to rolling round boulders down a thousand-fathom mountain. Such is the strategic configuration of power.[11]

The concept of the strategic configuration of power enunciated by Sun Tzu has received different interpretations by different scholars of military strategy. Suffice it to say that at its core, it refers to the latent power that a commander can conserve and that can be unleashed to maximum effect when needed.

The final broad strategic concept that can be gleaned from "The Art of War" is the idea of **unorthodox and orthodox**. Orthodox refers to doing things by the book, while the converse is unorthodox.

Sun Tzu's idea is that an astute general should have the flexibility and imagination to deploy his forces in unconventional ways when the need arises and deploy conventional tactics in unconventional ways to gain victory on the battlefield.

The Post-Sun Tzu Period

Sun Tzu still occupies a respectable position in contemporary discourse on military strategy. However, in the increasingly complex and technology-driven world, new challenges have emerged that cannot be effectively dealt with using Sun Tsu's military strategy. For example, new threats from non-state actors, such as the ideology-driven terrorist groups in multiple countries, the development of sophisticated armaments that can annihilate the earth several times over, and the internet's rapid development that creates new threats in cyberspace. These developments have necessitated a significant rethink of military strategy. A notable contemporary scholar in military strategy is Carl von Clausewitz. One of his famous works is "On War."

Biography of Carl von Clausewitz

Cal van Clausewitz was born in 1780 to a middle-class family in Burg, near Magdeburg, a town in what was then Prussia.[12]

He was the son of Friedrich Gabriel von Clausewitz, who served in the military as a lieutenant but subsequently became a tax collector. Clausewitz himself joined the army at 12, quite a young age by today's standards, but common practice during his time. He joined the army as a Lance Corporal and rose to the position of Major General several years later. [13]

He participated in several war campaigns before joining the German War School in 1801 at the age of 21. He was an exemplary student, earning the admiration of his tutors. He graduated in 1803 at the top of his class. [14]

After leaving college, Clausewitz participated in military combat, including the Battle of Jena-Auerstedt in 1806. He was captured along with 25,000 other soldiers and held hostage until 1807. (At that time in history, hostages were relatively free and had the freedom to move around.) [15]

Although relatively free, Clausewitz whined and groaned about his incarceration in France. He wrote his wife complaining that the French could not even cook and that what was supposed to be sour was sweet, and what was supposed to be sweet was sour. [16]

During his time in France, Clausewitz had the opportunity to witness first-hand and document the multiple instances and aspects of the mobilization of a country (France) into war.

He received parole in 1808 and returned to rejoin the Prussian army. For the next four years, Clausewitz worked on a broad array of military work, from strategy to the nitty-gritty of military operations, working for senior officers. [17]

However, Clausewitz was disillusioned by the Prussian army's kowtowing to Napoleon, and in 1812, he defected and joined the Russian army. He participated in various engagements, although his role was limited because he could not speak Russian.

He played a primarily advisory role and was even instrumental in the 1812 negotiations that led to the coalition of Prussia, Russia, and the United Kingdom that eventually defeated Napoleon. During all that time, Clausewitz continued to document his observations of the unfolding of war.

He rejoined the Russian army in 1815 as a colonel, rising to chief of staff shortly after that.

He was involved in several military engagements until his death from cholera in November 1831 at 51.

* * *

Clausewitz started writing the manuscript of his famous book, "On War," in 1816. He had not finished writing it by the time of his death. His widow, Marie von Clausewitz, edited the unfinished work and published it in 1832.

Clausewitz did not have much formal schooling. He is remembered for his tremendous gregariousness as a self-learner from a very early age. He was a great model of a lifelong autodidact learner. He was studying even when he was a prisoner in France. [18]

He read widely, covering engineering, mathematics, law, philosophy, and many other subjects. He was a true lover of knowledge.

His lack of a traditional education proved to be an advantage. This enabled him to create a certain freshness in his work.[19]

Snapshot of "On War"

Clausewitz wrote "On War" in German (first translated into English in 1874) over 12 years, initially as notes on everything about war. After that, he started reviewing and polishing the work. When writing the book, his original intention was that it would be read first by military analysts (theorists) and secondly by practitioners of war. The book was on the philosophy and practice of warfare.[20]

One of the key ideas he enunciated in the book was that war is a <u>continuation of policy by other means</u>. In other words, war aims to achieve political purposes. [21]

Below is an extract from the book.

War is nothing but a duel on a larger scale. Countless duels go to make up war, but a picture of it as a whole can be formed by imagining a pair of wrestlers. Each tries through physical force to compel the other to do his will; his immediate aim is to throw his opponent in order to make him incapable of further resistance. [22]

He also noted that there are two types of war: total war and limited war. Total war or absolute war is the type of war where the primary objective is total subjugation of the enemy using maximum pure unchecked violence—completely disarming the enemy so that he becomes completely bereft of any potential of posing a threat.

On the other hand, limited war is the war waged at the periphery using limited means to accomplish the objective, such as gaining territory or other assets that give you leverage for bargaining with the enemy. It can be waged without necessarily using violence.

Clausewitz emphasized that war is a highly complex phenomenon that requires critical thinking. He asserted that the education of military commanders was essential before they could engage in war.

Further, that battle was the decisive means to war success.

Clausewitz euphemistically noted that the whole purpose of the war was fighting. Like Sun Tzu, he pointed out that an act of war was intended to compel your enemy to do your will.

He described the concept of fog, or obscurity and friction. In other words, the unexpected was inevitable in a war. Anything can go wrong—for example, a change in weather conditions. Commanders must have the ability to handle such unexpected phenomena.

Clausewitz enunciated the principles of the psychological dominance of forces, the idea that the enemy is a living, thinking being susceptible to psychological manipulation. To put it in his language, the enemy has a vote.

Clausewitz defined war as a paradoxical trinity of primordial violence, hatred, and enmity. He said that these three ingredients must be present before a war can commence.

He also propounded the ideas of chance and probability (friction) inherent in war and reiterated that war was an instrument of government policy.

Although he talked about military strategy, most of what Clausewitz wrote was on the operational aspects of war.[23]

Thucydides

No matter how superficial, an overview of military strategy would be incomplete without mentioning the Thucydides and the Thucydides Trap. Some of his ideas are still relevant today and are cited by contemporary military strategy scholars. [24]

Biography of Thucydides

Thucydides was a military general born in Greece around 460 BC. He is famous amongst historians for being the earliest person to provide documentary evidence of historical events, notably his writings on the Peloponnesian War.

He wrote the first history and has been aptly described by some scholars as the father of history.[25]

Others consider Herodotus [c.490-420BC] the father of history. However, we will not dwell on this argument as it will distract us from our focus, namely, the origins of military strategy enunciated by Thucydides.

The Peloponnesian War

The Peloponnesian War between Sparta and Athens occurred between 431 and 404 BC. According to Thucydides, the war was primarily triggered by the rise of Athens, which Sparta interpreted as a threat to their superiority. To put it bluntly, Spartans became envious of the rapid rise of the Athenians. Therefore, they decided to launch a pre-emptive attack on Athens as a strategic way of curtailing their progress. To use Thucydides words:

It was the rise of Athens and the fear that this instilled in Sparta that made war inevitable.[26]

Historians have described this phenomenon as the "Thucydides Trap," a term coined by Graham Allison[27]. Contemporary literature on military strategy refers to the "Thucydides Trap" when discussing the US and China's current relations.[28,29]

In 1978, approximately nine out of every ten Chinese citizens survived on less than US$2 per day. In 2018, less than 1 in 100 Chinese citizens lived on less than $2 per day, and the number continues to shrink as the Chinese grow on all fronts. [30]

Braham Allison points out that during the past 500 years, there have been 16 cases of a rising power challenging an existing power. In 12 cases, the dominant power has waged war against the rising power. Because of this, some scholars worry that China's rapid rise could trigger hostilities and even war with the USA, which has become accustomed to being the dominant power in the 20th and 21st Centuries.

Some scholars suggest that the US could be gradually sliding into the "Thucydides Trap," going by its aggressive posture against China. [31,32]

CHAPTER 5

Game Theory

"You don't have to be a mathematician to have a feel for numbers."
—John Nash

THE WORD GAMES CONJURES UP images of playfulness. And it surely should. The ideas that are at the heart of it are fascinating concepts. Firstly, game theory teaches us that we constantly make game-theoretical moves daily. Secondly, it teaches us how to think strategically.

Overview of Game Theory

But what is game theory, one may ask? One of my favorite definitions is by Hank Green (2016).

Any interaction between multiple people in which each person's payoff is affected by the decisions made by others.[33]

Game theory was first pioneered as a mathematical concept by the noble laureate John Nash in 1950. Subsequently, it was extended to other disciplines, notably economics, biology, political science, military science, international relations, and strategy.

For example, economics used it to dispute a core principle advanced by Adam Smith which states that individuals acting in their self-interest invariably generate an economic equilibrium in society for humanity's common good. In other words, the economic system works as though it is directed by an invisible hand. To put it in Adam Smith's words:

Every individual necessarily labors to render the annual revenue of the society as great as he can ... He intends only his own security, and he is in this, as in many other cases, led by an invisible hand to promote an end which was no part of his intention ... By pursuing his own interests, he frequently promotes that of the society more effectually than when he really intends to promote it. I have never known much good done by those who affected to trade for the public good.[34]

This invisible hand metaphor was at the core of economic theory regarding the factors that drive supply and demand in free markets. However, from a game theory standpoint, this logic is slightly flawed. This can be demonstrated by the so-called prisoner's dilemma in game theory.

The Prisoner's Dilemma

Consider two friends, Kamau and Mutiso, who are involved in a crime. They were caught running away from a crime scene on the night of February 21, 2021.

The police do not have a watertight case against them. Still, the prosecutor believes he can nail them and obtain the maximum prison terms. However, he can only succeed if he gets one or both of them to confess.

Upon apprehension, the suspects (prisoners) are kept in two separate cells. The prisoners cannot communicate with each other at all. The prosecutor approaches Kamau's lawyer and makes the following plea bargain offer:

1. If your client confesses that he and Mutiso committed the crime, but Mutiso denies that he was involved, the judge will set your client free and jail Mutiso for the maximum sentence of ten years.
2. If, on the other hand, your client confesses and Mutiso confesses too, then both your client, Kamau, and Mutiso will go to jail, but for a lesser term of five years.

3. However, if both your client and Mutiso decline to confess, then each will go to jail for two years on a lesser charge because it will be difficult for the prosecution to establish a completely watertight case confirming the guilt for the more serious crime that the prosecution believes they have committed.

    The prosecutor makes a similar offer to Mutiso's lawyer.

Both prisoners are placed in a complicated dilemma. The best outcome for either of them is to go scot-free, but this can only happen if they confess and their partner in crime fails to confess. However, none of them can determine the action that their partner will take.

The second-best outcome is to go to jail for two years. And this can only happen if both prisoners fail to confess. However, this option is riddled with tremendous risk. If one of the prisoners assumes that their partner will not confess and decides not to confess, then if the partner takes the opposite action, the prisoner will go to jail for ten years, while the court will set free his partner.

So, the surest and best option for either prisoner is to confess because the worst that can happen to them is going to jail for five years, with the chance of going scot-free if their partner fails to confess.

In other words, by doing the most selfish thing, namely, confessing, the prisoners end up with a sub-optimal outcome: going to jail for five years. The ideal option for the partnership would be for both of them not to confess, in which case they would go to prison for only two years each. This goes counter to the Adam Smith metaphor of the invisible hand.

There are many other instances where the application of game theory shows less than an optimal outcome when people act in their self-interest.

Sonnenschein gives an example of an artist's depiction of several people at a dinner table. The table is full of sumptuous dishes. Each person is holding a long fork to pick up food from the table. However, because of the length of the fork, none of the diners can put food in their own mouth. However, by acting unselfishly and cooperating, diners on one side of the table can pick the food, feed their counterparts on the opposite side, and vice-versa.[35]

Engelhardt (2016) gives several examples from the field of entrepreneurship that illustrate the sub-optimality of decisions of individuals when perceived from a game theory perspective. One example is the use of public goods such as roads. In this instance, the choice that individuals face is whether to participate in the cost of public goods, such as roads, by paying taxes. If one does not pay taxes, but others pay, the person who does not pay taxes will enjoy a free resource at zero cost. If, on the other hand, one pays taxes, but others do not, then one will, in effect, cover the cost of a resource that free riders will enjoy.

As in the prisoner's dilemma case, the ideal situation would be for everyone to pay their taxes so that everyone can enjoy the resources developed by the government using taxes paid by everyone. However, the reality is that one cannot be sure that others will pay their fair share of taxes. Therefore, most individuals in this hypothetical scenario would prefer not to pay for the resource. Thus, the country will end up in a sub-optimal position where infrastructure becomes dilapidated because the government cannot collect taxes to pay for the resource.[36]

A Personal Example

At the time of writing, there is an ongoing discussion amongst residents in my neighborhood regarding erecting a security wall on one side of the estate to minimize the risk of intruders. A contractor has given a quotation of KShs 1.9 million to erect a robust concrete wall. Very soon, all residents will be required to contribute voluntarily towards this cost. The question that will arise in the minds of each resident will be as follows:

1. If all neighbors do the right thing and contribute towards the cost of the wall, we will build a good quality wall that will benefit everyone in the neighborhood.

2. If, on the other hand, I and a handful of other residents contribute, but the majority refuse to pay an equitable share, then the other few neighbors and I will feel cheated because we will have paid for a resource that will be enjoyed by everyone in the neighborhood including those who will not have made any contribution.

3. Alternatively, if most people feel free riders will take advantage of them, they will not contribute. Therefore, the funds collected will not cover the wall's construction cost. Accordingly, we will not be able to enhance security in the neighborhood.

Notice that the optimal solution for any resident (the Nash equilibrium) is: "not to contribute."[37] If others contribute enough to cover the cost, then the resident will enjoy a free resource. An absurd state of affairs, one might say!

You can probably think of numerous other prisoner dilemma scenarios.

But is that all that we can say about the prisoner's dilemma? The answer is "No." A strategic thinker can change the rules to attain the most beneficial outcome for all. For example, in the case of the neighborhood wall, one can lobby the local authority to impose a special mandatory levy to cover the cost of the wall. In that case, the avenue for free-riding will be closed, forcing everyone to contribute and enabling everyone to enjoy the benefit of a more secure neighborhood.

Competitive and Cooperative Games

There are two main branches of game theory: competitive and cooperative. In competitive games, there are some winners and some losers. The prisoner's dilemma is an example of a competitive strategy game.

Cooperative games are different because the best outcome is achieved when the participants cooperate. This occurs when the players form a coalition to achieve a common purpose, such as when countries decide to cooperate and share the cost of managing the potential challenges of climate change. The underlying idea is how to be fair with each other, unlike in competitive games, where everyone is trying to outmaneuver the other.

In cooperative games, the share of the value one gets from a coalition is called the Shapley value. This description comes from Lloyd Shapley (1951), who developed the methodology for calculating the most equitable contributions by coalition members in a cooperative game. An example will help illustrate the essence of a cooperative game.

Consider three individuals, Muthama, Kasuku, and Ndile, who are members of a church choir in Nairobi. They usually attend choir practice on Wednesday evenings, and each takes a taxi to and from their homes to the church.

Muthama has a bright idea. Instead of traveling separately, they could hire a taxi to carry them all from their homes to the church and back. Their homes are along the same route anyway.

Muthama lives 10 kilometers from the church and pays a taxi fare of KShs 1,200/= for a round trip. Kasuku lives a little further and pays KShs 1,600/= for a round trip. Ndile lives even further and pays KShs 2,200/=. So, in total, the three individuals spend KShs 5,000/= (1,200+ 1,600+ 2,200).

Going by Muthama's suggestion, the three of them can use just one taxi and pay a total cost of KShs 2,200/=, the fare that Ndile usually pays. The taxi will follow the route of the person who lives the furthest from the church, with the other riders joining or exiting the taxi en route.

The game theory question is: What is the fairest way of sharing the cost of KShs 2,200/=?

A simplistic way of distributing the cost would be to divide it by the ratio of the costs each person paid before deciding to use only one taxi. Using this method, Muthama would pay KShs 528 (i.e., 1,200/5,000 x 2,200); Kasuku would pay KShs 704 (i.e. 1,600/5,000 x 2,200); and Ndile would pay KShs 968 (i.e. 2,200/5,000 x 2,200).

However, using game theory methodology, that approach is not equitable. The distribution (called the Shapley value) should be Muthama KShs 400/=, Kasuku KShs 600/=, and Ndile KShs 1,200/=. The computation of the Shapley value is shown in Table 1.

Table 1: Computation of Shapley value

	Muthama	Kasuku	Ndile	Total
Individually	1,200	1,600	2,200	5,000

Coalitions	Muthama	Kasuku	Ndile	Total	Saving
Muthama, Kasuku, Ndile	1,200	400	600	2,200	2,800
Muthama, Ndile, Kasuku	1,200	0	1,000	2,200	2,800
Kasuku, Muthama, Ndile	0	1,600	600	2,200	2,800
Kasuku, Ndile, Muthama	0	1,600	600	2,200	2,800
Ndile, Muthama, Kasuku	0	0	2,200	2,200	2,800
Ndile, Kasuku, Muthama	0	0	2,200	2,200	2,800
Shapley value (Average)	400	600	1,200	2,200	2,800

A simplistic way of thinking about the coalitions is to assume that the three individuals pay for the taxi ride as they enter. For example, Muthama enters first and pays 1,200 to his destination. Kasuku enters next and pays 400, the remaining balance required to cover the fare of KShs 1,600 to his destination. Finally, Ndile enters the taxi and pays 600, the amount needed to cover the full fare of KShs 2,200 to his destination.

The other coalitions work precisely the same way, except for the sequence in which the three individuals enter the taxi. The Shapley value is computed as the average of the six coalitions (or sequences).

Several underlying axioms are assumed in deriving the Shapley value. A discussion of those axioms is beyond the scope of this book.

The example presented here is straightforward. The computations can be extremely complicated for different situations and are best left to game theory mathematicians.

However, from a strategy perspective, cooperative games demonstrate the need to think deeply about fairness in distributing the benefits that accrue from cooperation amongst participants.

Finite and Infinite Games

Games can also be classified as finite or infinite. The key characteristics of finite games include the inherent objective amongst the players of winning, externally defined rules that cannot be changed during play, and a temporal span within which the game is played to completion.

Finite games have specific boundaries. Every strategic move a player makes in such a game is intended to enhance the player's chances of winning. Any move that does not drive this purpose is redundant.

Examples of finite games are board games and Olympic sports such as basketball, soccer, and tennis. Other finite games in the military sphere are military campaigns, wars, and battles. Other interactions between people that would be classified as finite games are court cases and debates.[38]

Infinite games, on the other hand, are continuous. They do not have a predetermined endpoint. The players internally define the rules and can change them at any time. The strategy of such games is to sustain continuity over the distant horizon. An example is a career in a particular profession. When considering a career, they aim for longevity, not short-term wins. In contrast, a job interview is a finite game. In this instance, the strategy is to come out the winner amongst a group of interviewees and get hired for the job.[39]

Carse (2013) first articulated the ideas around finite and infinite games. Carse argued that strategy problems emerge when decisions with implications for the long term are treated as finite games. Sinek (2017) gives several examples.

When the United States fought in Vietnam, they fought a finite game with clear-cut short-term objectives. The Americans couldn't declare victory since the Vietcong were in it for the long haul, essentially fighting for their lives – an infinite game.

The same thing happened in Afghanistan when the Soviet Union fought the Mujahedeen. The latter were fighting for their lives, yet the Soviets aimed for short-term victory. The Soviets ran out of resources and abandoned the war effort out of frustration.

Sinek (2017) argues that the Cold War between the United States and the Soviet Union was an infinite game that is still raging. However, the United States made a strategic blunder by declaring victory in 1989 when the Berlin Wall collapsed – as if the Cold War was a finite game.

Sinek points out that the Cold War is ongoing, even if the Soviet Union is not the main protagonist. He argues that the Cold War with the Soviet Union was based on a desire for military superiority on three fronts: nuclear armaments, ideology, and economics. But this was subsequently replaced by renewed tensions with the emergence of new powers that possessed nuclear weapons and new ideologies (e.g., Islamic extremism.) According to Sinek, the blunder by the Americans in declaring victory created uncertainty and chaos that are still plaguing the world to this day.[40]

Sinek further argues that companies make similar strategic mistakes by adopting short-term strategies aimed at winning in the short term and then getting frustrated when their rivals who play the long-term infinite game continue to survive without being affected by short-term disruptions.

$$* \quad * \quad *$$

There is much more to game theory than we have reviewed in these few pages. The idea was to present some basic concepts to open our minds to different ways of thinking strategically.

A Word on John Nash

From time to time, there is a new entrant on the world stage who makes such a considerable impact on humanity that it mesmerizes everyone. John Nash, the inventor of game theory, was one such individual.

He was so bright that Richard Duffin, Nash's undergraduate advisor at the Carnegie Institute of Technology, wrote a letter of support to John Nash's application to attend the Ph.D. program at Princeton University, which became famous for its exceptionally pointed conciseness. Matthews (1915) described it as the best letter of recommendation ever. It read as follows:

"Dear Professor Lefschetz:
This is to recommend Mr. John F. Nash, Jr., who has applied for entrance to the graduate college at Princeton.
Mr. Nash is nineteen years old and is graduating from Carnegie Tech in June. He is a mathematical genius.
Yours sincerely,
Richard J. Duffin"[41]

John Nash completed his Ph.D. program at Princeton University at 21. His Ph.D. thesis, Non-cooperative Games, was a mere 27 pages, including the bibliography and acknowledgments.[42] The bibliography contained only two sources.

According to Google Scholar, the thesis had been cited 12,004 times as of February 7, 2021.[43]

John Nash and his wife died in a tragic car accident on May 23, 2015. Sylvia Nasar tells John Nash's incredible story in a biography entitled "A Beautiful Mind."[44] The story is relived in the award-winning film of the same name, starring Richard Crowe.[45]

PART III

ESSENTIAL ELEMENTS OF STRATEGY

CHAPTER 6

Enter Akili Mali

*"Growth is never by mere chance; it is the result of
forces working together."*
— James Cash Penney

A KILI MALI COULD NOT BELIEVE the unexpected turn
of events. He had agreed to take over the fledgling
Sukuma Wiki Pet Shop, including its stock-in-trade
and a gradually withering image, at a bargain price of only
KShs 2 million. He was confident that he could quickly turn
it around. He had come to this conclusion after performing a
high-level industry analysis.[46]

To start with, there were very few shops in Nairobi that
were fully dedicated to pet foods. Pet foods were sold mainly
in supermarkets, typically in a pet food section at the furthest
corner end of the store.

Secondly, although pet owners could use homemade food, they preferred to procure prepared pet food in supermarkets; the exception was pet owners in the less affluent parts of the city, such as Kawangware. Many such people typically fed their pets on leftovers. For such people, buying food for dogs and cats in the supermarket was a sign of snobbishness, a proclivity of the rich who had long forgotten the value of money. This was a customer segment that Akili Mali could ignore for the time being.

Many dogs loafed around Kawangware village. But to an aspiring seller of pet foods, that phenomenon was a mirage. Most of those dogs were dogs without a life. Dogs that had never tasted a well-prepared dog meal and did not have the slightest chance of ever eating a well-balanced diet. They were dogs owned by people of meager means.

There were a few lucky dogs in the neighborhood. They had relatively well-to-do owners, but many rarely fed them pet food from the shops.

The place was hardly visited by the suburbanites who valued their pets and could afford good quality pet foods.

Accordingly, the big problem Akili Mali needed to solve quickly was the urgent relocation of the Sukuma Wiki Pet Foods Shop from Kawangware. It was precisely the wrong place for such a business.

Akili Mali had also discovered that most buyers of pet foods were not sensitive to prices. The majority were in the middle-income group and above who occasionally visited the pet food section in supermarkets to buy items for stocking up in their homes.

Another critical fact Akili Mali established was that several pet food manufacturers in Nairobi competed in supermarkets. Almost all supermarkets enjoyed significant discounts and received extended credit from pet food manufacturers.

Also, very few people appeared to run shops that specialized in pet food only. He believed that Sukuma Wiki may have seen that market opportunity but could not exploit it effectively.

Positioning the Business

Akili Mali was alive to four realities that he had learned in business school. Firstly, a good position in a healthy industry meant excellent profitability. A bad position in a healthy industry meant mediocre profitability. A good position in an unhealthy industry meant mediocre profitability. And a bad position in an unhealthy industry meant poor profitability.[47]

Akili Mali was entering a reasonably healthy industry with the potential for success. The same could not be said of the manufacturing side of pet foods, where the competition was stiff. But he did not want to go there for the time being.

He just needed to position his business properly relative to other players in the industry, mainly supermarkets. He also had to do whatever it took to gain a competitive advantage, which would not be easy.

Firstly, the stock he had inherited from Sukuma Wiki consisted of standard, run-of-the-mill items that could be found in any supermarket. He could only gain an edge over others by importing high-quality foods that could not be found in Nairobi supermarkets.

He had done some research to determine the types of imported foods stocked in supermarkets. Most of the imports were generic brand names from the Far East. He decided to go a notch higher and import the branded products from South Africa, Europe, and America.

He was taking a considerable risk because imported pet foods were more expensive than locally manufactured foods. However, he would overcome that disadvantage by charging premium selling prices for the products. He would also support the prices with strong marketing campaigns and other initiatives. And he had a few tricks up his sleeve to accomplish this purpose.

Akili Mali knew he had to develop a unique value proposition to differentiate his products and services from supermarkets. This would be the surest way of quickly gaining a foothold in the market. He would still implement initiatives to ensure operational excellence, but differentiation would be his key focus.

Offering Unique Value

A few days after signing the contract with Sukuma Wiki, Akili Mali visited all the shopping centers and malls in Nairobi's high-end suburbs.

He was lucky. He found an empty shop in one of the high-end malls. The monthly rental was KShs 100,000/=, but he was willing to take the risk of transferring the business from Kawangware to the Mall.

Akili Mali borrowed KShs 1 million from a local bank to help him furnish the new shop and increase his pet food inventory with imported high-quality items.

But what would be his unique value proposition, Akili Mali pondered? The answer to this question would be critical for laying a solid foundation for his new business venture.

After many hours of careful thought, Akili Mali decided that his unique value would be:

To proactively identify and fulfill the nutrition needs of pets in the Karen suburb and other similar neighborhoods in Nairobi using professional, personalized customer service.

To this end, Akili Mali hired a veterinarian who had just graduated from university. Her primary role was to use all means available to identify and document all pets and owners in the neighborhood. Further, she proactively reached out to pet owners using various avenues and provided them with nutritional information for their pets. Additionally, she offered one-month free follow-up nutritional advice. She also recommended an annual regimen of pet food and other supplies.

Akili Mali would guarantee free food and supplies delivery when needed based on a pre-agreed schedule. As a complimentary service, Akili Mali would offer pet owners 24-hour emergency veterinary services.

Akili Mali's goal was to capture 30% of the pet foods market in Nairobi's high-end suburbs within three years.

He instructed his employees to focus on the target pet owners' group in Nairobi's high-end suburbs. While exceptionally few customers from Kawangware and other areas would not be ignored, they would not be the Akili Mali business's primary focus.

His typical target customer profile was a retired lady or gentleman who lived on premises with a large garden and possessed three pets - usually two dogs and a cat. The dog premises would be well-designed kernels located several meters from the main house, near the servant's quarters. He employed a worker whose only responsibility was to feed the dogs, take them for morning walks, and wash them at the end of the day. The premises would typically have the owner's name shown on a small signboard in front of the gate. Typical names of such customers were Mr. Fort Knox, Dr. Washington Moneybags, Mr. Osman Mapesa, Mr. Justus Gitonga, Mrs. Agnes Purecash, Mr. Edington Zeroworries, Mrs. Currency Biggs, Ms. Diamonds R. Forever, Mr. Forex Plenty, Bwana CBK Kamau Mbeca, Mr. Greenbacks Euros, Mrs. Nomoney Blues, Mr. Tha Mint, Ms. Gifted Passons, Dr. Goldfinger Edwards, Ms. Chums Unlimited.

On a field visit to one of the suburbs with Akili Mali's sales girls, a pet food consultant from Germany had asked Akili Mali why it seemed that most of the customers had the name Mbwa Kali. The question was amusing, but the answer offered valuable insights into the profile of the clientele Akili Mali was targeting.

Mbwa Kali means vicious dog in Kiswahili. Many of Akili Mali's clients had a sign with these words prominently displayed at their gate to warn would-be intruders that vicious dogs were on the premises.

That situation sharply contrasted with the customer landscape in Kawangware, the original home of Sukuma Wiki Pet Shop. A Kawangware customer would typically be a junior employee in a company or government office who lived in rented quarters and owned one dog locked in a small ramshackle structure built outside the front of the house. The dog was typically used as a security alarm to inform the owner of visitors or unwanted intruders. Such a dog was fed on domestic leftovers or meatless bones from a nearby butchery. Typical names of such customers were Wololo Yaee, Naisaruru Ole Sumbua, Washington McGeorge Butbroke, Alphonse Kulawaya, Sinapesa Yakutosha, Wasiwasi Jamaa, Kula Bilakulipa, Ugali Bilamboga, Wanyonyi Munyonyaji, Masumbuko Kilasiku, Jackton Nomoney Ochieng, Alistuka Kwakukosamali, Hatasupu Hamna, Wali Wakudoea, Maringo Bilapesa, Gutiri Mbeca, Shetani Ashindwe, Suruali Mojapekee, and Pesa Onge.

For Kiswahili speakers, the pun in the customer names is intended to drive home a key point in strategy: the importance of customer segmentation.

The German consultant was also intrigued by the family ties evident from the names of several shops he saw on his way to the mall. The most striking thing was that the names of businesses run by indigenous Kenyans seemed to espouse brotherly love. In contrast, names of shops run by Asians seemed to project a more paternal angle.

Indigenous Kenyans had business names such as Kamau and Brothers, Muthengi and Brothers, Onyango, Otieno, and Brothers. Asian businesses, on the other hand, had such names as Patel and Sons, PJ Shah and Sons, and Babujee and Sons. However, the consultant learned from Akili Mali that such business names most likely had nothing to do with family ties but business image and a dash of creativity.

Akili Mali hired two beautiful sales girls who attended mandatory customer service training and a basic animal husbandry course. The girls were responsible for ensuring the shop was always kept in tip-top, clean condition.

Akili Mali also launched a blog on the internet to communicate with his customers and other stakeholders.

Every customer who made a purchase at the Akili Mali pet food shop was given a flier. The flier contained pertinent information regarding pet care, including items they could procure from the shop, either physically by visiting the shop or ordering online for same-day home delivery.

Akili Mali implemented various other initiatives to improve operating effectiveness. For example, he introduced a mandatory daily meeting for all staff members at 8:30 a.m. to review performance for the previous day and plan activities for the day. He introduced a personal performance tracker for every employee, which formed the basis of the daily briefings.

Because of the enhanced business model that Akili Mali had deployed, pet products were sold at a premium compared to those in supermarkets. This pricing approach put off some customers, especially those from Kawangware and other similar areas. However, incremental revenue from the higher-priced products sold to customers from the high-end suburbs offset the loss in the number of customers.

* * *

The Akili Mali Pet Shop recorded losses during the first six months. The losses were primarily due to the high start-up costs and the aggressive marketing and sales promotion activities.

The losses were not a big concern to Akili Mali. They were in line with his financial projections.

In the eighth month, the business turned and started making profits. By the end of the year, the company broke even.

By the end of the second year, Akili Mali made enough money to afford a substantial refurbishment of the shop.

Akili Mali started expanding his business to other malls by the fourth year.

By the fifth year, Akili Mali was in all the up-market malls in Nairobi. The company was growing rapidly. The sky was the limit!

CHAPTER 7

Knowledge is Power

*"I did then what I knew how to do. Now that I
know better, I do better. "
— Maya Angelou*

THERE IS A GOOD REASON why people pay thousands of dollars to join business schools. The annual cost of an MBA program in some of the most reputable business schools globally ranges from around US$ 100,000 to 150,000.[48] A good grounding in business education in such schools gives one an edge over others in the world of business. This is not to say that those who do not attend business school cannot succeed in business. The point is that ideas taught in business schools can make a big difference in business. Some of those business ideas relate to strategy.

* * *

Michael Porter

One of the doyens of strategy is Michael Porter. He graduated from Princeton University with degrees in aerospace and mechanical engineering. He then attended Harvard Business School for postgraduate studies, where he graduated at the top of his class in the MBA program. He earned a Ph.D. in business economics from the same university in 1973 and became a professor at Harvard Business School. [49]

Michael Porter is renowned for his groundbreaking work on strategy, notably his highly publicized article entitled "The Five Forces that Shape Strategy," first published in the March/April 1979 edition of the Harvard Business Review. He is also one of the founders of the Monitor Group consultancy firm. [50]

Porter's Five Forces Model

According to Porter (1979), a company's profitability is a function of its position in an industry. Further, an industry's attractiveness is based on five factors that affect firms operating in that industry. These are rivalry amongst firms in that industry, the threat of substitute products, customers' bargaining power, suppliers' bargaining power, and the threat of new entrants. [51]

Figure 2 shows a graphical illustration of Porter's Five Forces model.[52] This is an excellent starting point for gaining a deep understanding of strategy.

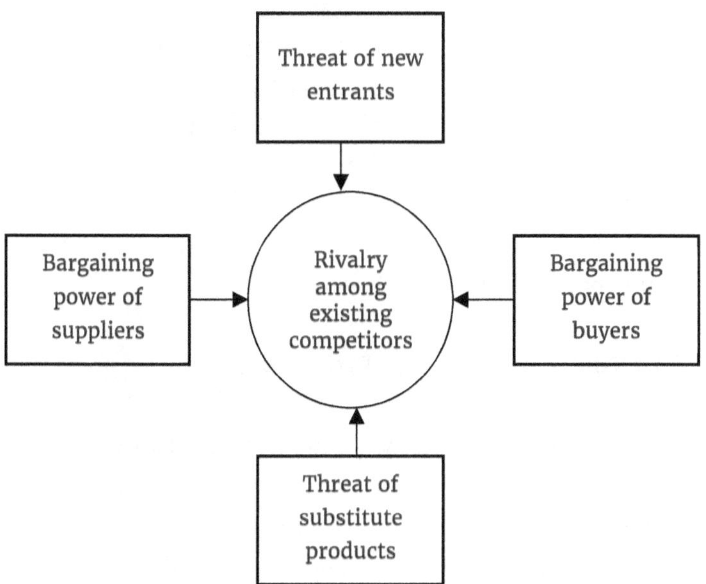

Figure 2: The five forces that shape strategy

Competition Among Existing Competitors

If competition amongst firms in an industry is too intense, the individual firms' profitability will likely remain low. That is because of the constant downward pressure on prices as firms try to outdo each other.

An example of this phenomenon is the horticultural crops business in Kenya. During the rainy season, the market is usually flooded with different vegetables, forcing prices down to rock bottom levels.

If you wish to have a first-hand experience of the force of rivalry amongst competitors, drive to Soko Mjinga market near View-point, 15 kilometers from Kimende town in Kiambu county, one Saturday morning. As your vehicle gradually comes to a stop, you will be surrounded by multiple vegetable vendors. Each of them will make an effort to sell you their produce. You may find it quite annoying if you have never been there before. But if you think of it as a manifestation of one of Porter's five forces, you will be immensely intellectually fulfilled.

The Threat of Substitute Products

If customers can easily switch to substitute products, firms in the industry will always be at the mercy of customers. Profitability is, therefore, likely to remain subdued because of the potential competition from substitutes. An example is in the passenger transport industry. Owners of *matatus* (small vans) do not have much leeway in setting prices because customers can easily switch from matatus to buses or even trains.

Bargaining Power of Customers

If an industry depends on a few powerful customers, then the customers will dictate prices, making it difficult for firms in that industry to make big profits. The coffee industry in developed countries is a case in point.

Unprocessed coffee produced in developing countries, such as Kenya, is purchased by a handful of powerful global commodity trading companies. These companies dictate the buying prices, making the unprocessed coffee industry one of the most unprofitable sectors globally.[53]

Bargaining Power of Suppliers

A similar phenomenon exists if firms in an industry depend on a few powerful suppliers. In this case, the suppliers will dictate the prices of inputs, making it difficult for the firms to operate at profitable margins. An example is the beverage business, where soft drink bottlers depend on a few powerful suppliers for beverage bases.

The Threat of New Entrants

Finally, if there are few barriers to entering the industry, new competitors can easily jump into the industry. The new entrants will intensify competition, drive down prices, and force firms into a downward spiral of low profitability. Once again, the *matatu* business in Kenya is an excellent example of this phenomenon. Almost anyone who can afford a van can get into this business. This ease of entry has led to a proliferation of *matatus* in the country, with the attendant low profitability of most industry players (except in places where some *matatu* owners have formed cartels that use mafia-like tactics to create barriers to prevent potential new entrants).

* * *

The industry analysis described above should be a good starting point for anyone who wishes to start a new business. Sukuma Wiki, who ended up languishing in misery, clearly did not diligently analyze the industry before starting his Pet Food business venture. The consequences of that omission were painful.

On the contrary, Akili Mali carefully analyzed and obtained insights that helped him decide how to position his business for success.

Alternative Perspectives

Various alternative models have been developed to explain the factors that drive strategy and the attendant firm profitability. Many such models supplement the ideas advanced by Porter (1979). Barney (1991) promulgated one such model: the Resource-Based View (RBV).[54]

The Resource-Based View (RBV)

RBV is an "inside-out" perspective of strategic factors, as contrasted to Porter's (1979) "outside-in" perspective. In other words, RBV looks at strategy based on a firm's internal resource endowment and how the resources manifest as competitive advantages in an industry or amongst its direct competitors.

According to Barney (1991), there are four attributes of a resource that create a competitive advantage for a firm: the value of the resource, its rarity (i.e., how rare it is), and its immutability (i.e., how difficult it is to imitate), and its substitutability (i.e., how difficult it is to find substitutes). The four attributes of resources can also be described as the idiosyncrasies or the firm's internal characteristics.

The four attributes are a function of their heterogeneity (i.e., how diverse they are within an industry) and immobility (i.e., how easily they can be moved). The Barney RBV model is depicted in Figure 3.

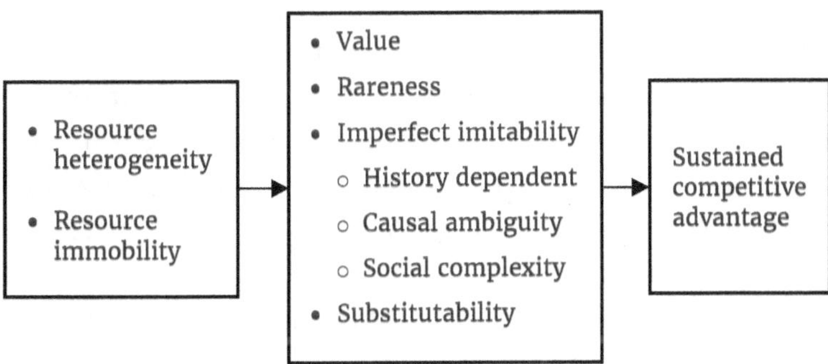

Figure 3: The Resource-Based View of strategy

Some terminologies used here may be intimidating, but the concepts are relatively easy to grasp.

By resources, Barney refers to all the different types of resources a firm might possess.

The resources include plant and machinery, unique processes developed over time, valuable information, relationships amongst employees, relationships with outsiders, staff training, geographic location, experience, organizational structures, and capabilities (i.e., expertise in doing certain things). The list is almost endless. The resources can be classified into physical, human, and organizational.

One way of easily understanding what Barney means by resource heterogeneity and resource immobility is to think of the opposites of these terms.

If resources within an industry were homogeneous, then it is unlikely that any firm could gain a competitive advantage from those resources. But there are exceptions. For example, a firm can move first and gain a first-mover advantage in the early stages (e.g., locking in customers, building a reputation, etc.), although such an advantage may only be short-lived. But let us not muddy the waters by getting into such nuances.

The other point is that if resources are mobile, they could hardly be a competitive advantage since other firms could easily acquire them.

So, as we think of strategy based on the four attributes (value, rarity, imitability, and substitutability), we should not lose sight of these pre-conditions (heterogeneity and immobility).

With these basic assumptions behind us, let's explore Barney's four attributes of sustainable competitive advantage in more detail.

Value

One analogy to explain value as a competitive advantage relates to Football Clubs. In 2020, the Real Madrid Football Club could afford to pay Eden Hazard slightly over US$720,000 per week because of his tremendous value to the team. Gareth Bale was close behind with a weekly salary of US$690,000.[55]

In comparison, Kenya's two highest-paid football club players earned around US$ 900 each.[56]

So, if you were Real Madrid's owner, you would have a much better chance of earning large sums of money from TV viewership than the owner of any football club in Kenya. So, in the context of global football, Real Madrid has a significant competitive advantage over Kenyan football clubs. However, that may not necessarily be the case from the European football industry's perspective. Several European clubs have valuable players, such as Eden Hazard and Gareth Bale, in their stable.

Rarity

Perhaps one of the strongest sources of competitive advantage is the possession of a rare resource. You are home and dry if you discover a gold mine behind your backyard (and nobody else sells gold in the country) - assuming the law would allow you to prospect the gold for personal use.

In some jurisdictions, anything below a few feet underground belongs to the government, even if it is in your backyard. That is partly why, in Kenya, people who sink boreholes in their premises require government agencies' permits and pay periodic rates for extracting water from the ground. So, if you discover Tanzanite in your vegetable garden, you may want to hesitate before you go merry-making. The discovery may not give you any competitive advantage.

However, rarity does not refer only to physical resources. If you start a business in the music industry, the talented musicians you may have in your stable may be a tremendous competitive advantage. Just imagine if Beyonce Knowles or Burna Boy were on your team. You would, in essence, be the owner of a mint – right there.

Imitability

The advantage of possessing a resource that cannot be easily imitated should be intuitively apparent.

Huawei pioneered 5G technology, which is not easy to replicate. A few countries that have been unable to develop similar technology and feel threatened by Huawei have blocked Huawei technology from being marketed in their countries.

Another example is the formula for Coca-Cola. This formula has given the Coca-Cola Company an enduring competitive advantage for decades.

Three factors can make a resource difficult to imitate: historical factors, causal ambiguity, or social complexity. A historical factor could be a culture that has emerged within the firm rooted in its founding at a particular time in history. Causal ambiguity refers to when the competitors cannot quite understand the configuration of a particular resource. Social complexity refers to the social networks built by an organization, its corporate culture, and other unique social dynamics a firm possesses.

Industry Health and Resource Endowment

Figure 4 summarizes the drivers of profitability-based ideas by Porter (1979) on industry health determinants and the Resource-Based View on sustainable competitive advantage propounded by Barney (1991).

Various other variations of these models have emerged in more recent years. Still, the basic constructs developed by Porter and Barney remain mostly unchanged.

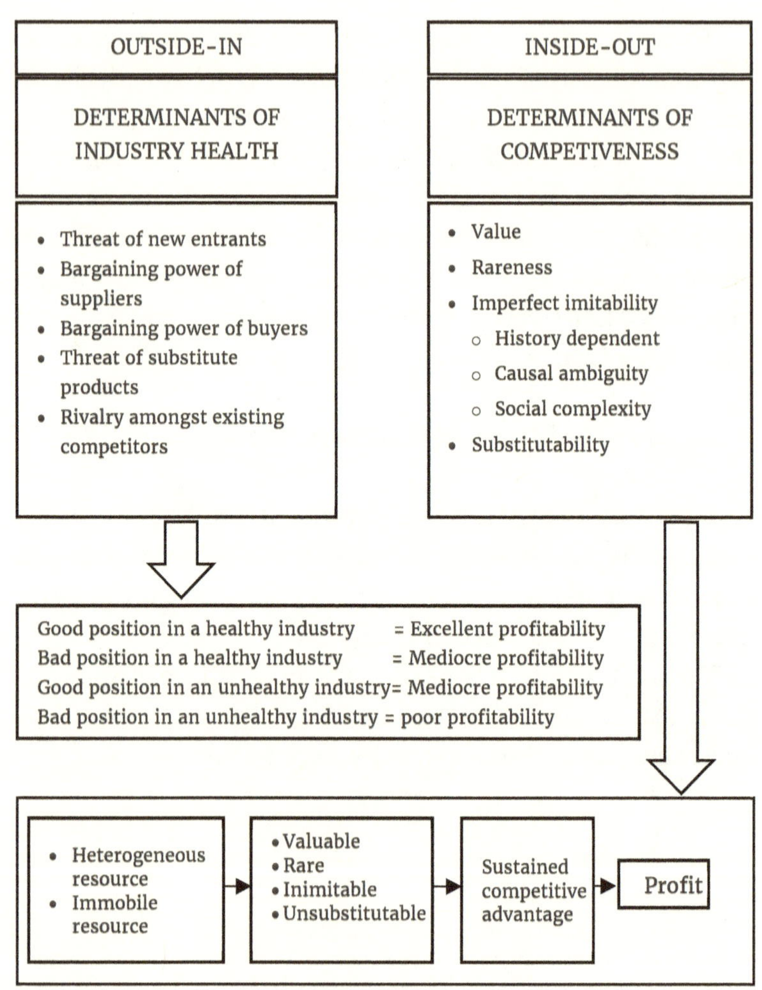

Figure 4: Determinants of profitability

CHAPTER 8

Differentiation

"Be faithful to that which exists nowhere but in yourself- and thus make yourself indispensable. "
—André Gide

Everyone who runs a business or leads another type of organization tries to do their best to increase their respective organization's profitability or value. Indeed, if all the world strategy practitioners were to do an excellent job, the world would become a much better place. All organizations would occupy unique positions in the universe and add value in their unique way. That would, in the aggregate, result in a more prosperous world.

* * *

The Basic Economic Model

The basic economic model of any enterprise is straightforward. It boils down to two things: revenues and costs. The difference between these two things is the profit or the economic value generated by the enterprise.

$$\text{Revenues} - \text{Costs} = \text{Profits}$$

This simple equation is valid in almost any organization, whether or not a profit motive drives it. For so-called non-profits, there is always a value proposition of some sort. The proposition could be as abstract as promoting the well-being of a particular social group.

With appropriate diligence, any organization's overriding objective can be reduced to specific values, as represented by the basic economic model shown above.

In other words, the basic idea is always to optimize the left-hand side of the equation. By doing so, the right-hand side of the equation will automatically take care of itself. Humanity can maximize society's collective well-being by taking short—and long-term actions to optimize the left-hand side of the equation.

Ignoring the essence of this fundamental truth is the surest path to economic and, I dare add, social ruin.

As we continue developing a strategic mindset, it is wise to keep this simple model in mind.

A Caveat

Of course, the model presented above is very simplistic. There are a gazillion things that go behind each of the three variables of the equation. For example, accountants will go to the extremes of explaining what should legitimately be described as revenue, cost, or profit. They will talk about the materiality of the amounts involved based on the context. They will also speak of these things in the temporal dimension. For instance, you will hear them say that a shilling received or spent today has a different value from a shilling received or spent six months from today. They will also cite all manner of rules that guide the determination of revenues and costs to ensure unanimity in the interpretation of the numbers.

Economists, some of whom have an unparalleled capacity to mesmerize and obfuscate, will tell you that costs have a certain magical power of increasing profits. If this sounds surprising, it is, and it is also true.

Keynesian economists will say that during an economic depression, the best course of action to revitalize an economy is to increase government spending. In other words, let the government go haywire in spending, and *voila*, the spending will trigger the production of goods and services. The production activity will, in turn, increase money in people's pockets and spur consumer demand for goods and services.

And through some *abracadabra*, consumer demand will translate into revenues for manufacturers, who will make a lot of money. And the economic engine will, through some invisible magic, start cranking away once again.

This idea may sound humorous to non-economists, but it works like a charm. It is one of the most critical tools multiple governments have used for decades, with impressive economic and social results.

The point we are making here is that there is some underlying complexity behind the model that may not be visible to many ordinary mortals - a complexity that we will ignore in our quest to develop a strategic mindset.

As strategists, we often need to think BIG PICTURE. And you will be surprised by the effectiveness of adopting such a big-picture approach.

Back to the Basic Economic Model

If we start from the premise that economic endeavors (and most noneconomic endeavors) are driven by the basic model (i.e., Revenues − Cost = Profit), we can build on the preceding chapter to elucidate how the model applies from a strategy standpoint. To this end, we will dive into a core strategy concept developed by Porter (1996).[57]

The idea is so fundamental that if it were the only concept the reader grasps in this book, the author's objective would have been substantially fulfilled. The idea has its roots in economics: differentiation.

We will cover the concept in small strides to ensure you grasp it completely.

Operating Effectiveness

Perhaps the most intuitive way of thinking about firm performance is that it is maximized when we work hard to increase revenues and minimize costs. But if we step back and ask ourselves how we can accomplish this purpose, a few things come to mind.

One of the first ideas that may pop up in one's mind is how to improve operating effectiveness to minimize costs and increase profits. Remember our basic economic model: Revenues − Costs = Profits.

There is no argument that by putting a lot of effort into improving the second variable of this equation (i.e., Costs), we automatically increase our profitability. But wait a minute. Is that all that we can do to improve profitability? The answer is "No."

We can also do multiple things to improve the first variable of the equation, namely Revenues. For example, we can produce more products to ensure that we never run out of supplies and never miss an opportunity to fulfill demand. We can also increase package sizes so that customers buy more volumes of our products, which would increase our revenues and positively impact profits.

However, Porter (2019) states that we can achieve superior results by thinking and acting differently.

Differentiation

We should start by considering that we are not the only ones supplying products to customers in the market. If we put on this strategy thinking hat, we will realize that the best chance in a competitive landscape is to differentiate ourselves from our competitors. In other words, we should strive to be unique and offer customers products or services that they will perceive as more valuable than those of our competitors.

We should pursue differentiation with laser focus so that our customers will always default to our products instead of choosing our competitors' products.

We still need to enhance our operating effectiveness, but the key idea is to do our best to be unique.

The quest for uniqueness could have a cost, forcing us to raise our prices above our competitors. But that would be fine if we could win the hearts and minds of our customers by doing so. In the long run, our incremental cost arising from differentiation would be offset by the incremental revenue we would earn due to differentiating ourselves from competitors.

Also, the quantities we sell may drop. Once again, the shortfall in quantity would likely be offset by the incremental revenue we would realize by charging a premium price.

Unique Value Proposition

In a nutshell, our approach would be to create a unique value proposition that would involve answering key strategic questions. Firstly, who are our target customers? Secondly, what are their needs? Thirdly, what distinctive approach can we use to fulfill those needs? Fourthly, what price should we charge for the unique value embedded in the product or service?

We would gain a competitive advantage over other market players and profitability by answering these four questions and acting accordingly.

Example

Let us explore these differentiation ideas using a simple example: dry dog food that sells for KShs 100 per packet.

Let us keep things simple and assume that the total cost per packet is KShs 40 (i.e., costs of buying the product from the manufacturer, storage, distribution, and other costs directly attributable to the product). That means that for every packet sold, the business makes a profit of KShs 60.

Per Packet	KShs
Selling price	100
Cost	40
Profit	60

Below is a table showing the profitability of the business under the status quo, where the average sales for one month total 1,000 packets, and under different scenarios in which the company implements measures to enhance operating effectiveness or implements strategies to differentiate the product against the competition (e.g., through superior secondary packaging, home delivery, personalized customer service, and advertising).

Table 2: Profitability under different scenarios

Scenarios	Qty	Revenues			Costs		Profit
		Per Unit	Revenue		Per unit	Cost	
	A	B	C=AxB		D	E=AxD	C-E
1. Status quo	1,000	100.00	100,000.00		40.00	40,000.00	60,000.00
2. With differentiation	900	120.00	108,000.00		40.00	36,000.00	72,000.00
3. With differentiation	1,000	120.00	120,000.00		40.00	40,000.00	80,000.00
4. With operating effectiveness	1,000	100.00	100,000.00		20.00	20,000.00	80,000.00
5. With differentiation and operating effectiveness	900	120.00	108,000.00		20.00	18,000.00	90,000.00
6. With differentiation and operating effectiveness	1,000	120.00	120,000.00		20.00	20,000.00	100,000.00

In the status quo scenario, the business makes a profit of KShs 60,000 during the month.

By implementing differentiation strategies, the company can charge a premium price for the product (i.e., KShs 120 instead of the regular price of KShs 100).

However, this change would cause a drop in sales quantities in the initial stages, from 1,000 to 900 packets. But notice that despite the decline in quantity, the profit increases from KShs 60,000 to KShs 72,000.

However, even after implementing the differentiation strategies and charging a premium price for the dog food, the quantity sold may remain at previous levels. This outcome is a real possibility, given that the target consumer group may be in the high-income bracket. In this instance, the business's profitability would rise to KShs 80,000.

On the other hand, if the company did not implement any differentiation strategies but focused on enhancing operating effectiveness, the sales quantities would most likely remain at normal levels.

The company would be able to improve its profitability through the reduction of costs. In our example, the cost per unit would drop from Kshs 40 to KShs 20, resulting in KShs 80,000 profit.

If the company did both things, namely, implementing differentiation strategies and implementing initiatives to improve operating effectiveness (assuming that the quantity dropped due to premium pricing), then the company would make a higher profit (KShs 90,000).

Finally, if the company did both things but the quantity at remained at the same level, the profit would be even higher (KShs 100,000).

It is conceivable that with differentiation strategies and improved operating effectiveness, the quantity could increase beyond normal levels, resulting in even higher profits for the company.

The numbers in the above example are fictitious but should drive home a key point: **differentiation is at the core of a winning strategy**.

Developing a unique value proposition is the critical starting point for successfully growing the business. By overlaying this with ongoing operating effectiveness initiatives, one is bound to achieve superior business results.

Indeed, if all businesses in an industry pursue this approach, the chances are that the overall pie in the industry would grow bigger, and everyone in the industry would prosper.

PART IV

STRATEGY THEORY

CHAPTER 9

The Big Picture of Strategy

"Instead of thinking outside the box, get rid of the box."
— Deepak Chopra

THE STORIES ABOUT SUKUMA WIKI AND AKILI MALI, hopefully gave the reader a glimpse of the enormous difference that strategy can make to one's business and life. It can prevent an expensive, unplanned dinner with one's spouse to nurse the wounds of an unsuccessful business venture. Instead, good strategies can take one to an exciting place where personal growth would be almost limitless. Strategy and strategic thinking pay.

* * *

This chapter will explore the big picture of strategy in business and introduce some popular terminologies strategy practitioners use.

Some of the material will be pretty theoretical. Still, it helps build one's ability to communicate effectively with strategy practitioners.

* * *

Several years ago, I joined a team rolling out a major ERP system. During the first few days, I attended project meetings but could not make head or tail of what the ERP technical consultants were saying. They seemed to have been speaking in an IT language that only they and perhaps some aliens from the Andromeda galaxy could understand. The Andromeda galaxy is twice the size of our Milky Way, so the people there must be twice as smart as us earthly non-ERP mortals. It was an immensely frustrating experience.

Fortunately, my employer had lined up training for the team. After the training, everything fell into place nicely. I started enjoying participating in team meetings.

In my later career in business strategy, I could not help feeling sympathy for colleagues who found themselves in almost similar situations. The following pages aim to equip readers with valuable knowledge to ensure they are never uncomfortable in any strategy conversation.

CORPORATE, BUSINESS, AND FUNCTIONAL STRATEGIES

As a starting point, it is important to crystallize our understanding of the different levels of strategy. This area may be a little foggy for many strategy field newcomers.

Figure 5 shows a high-level depiction of the three levels of the strategy framework.

Figure 5: The three levels of strategy

CORPORATE STRATEGY

Corporate strategy is the highest level of strategy. One easy way of thinking about it is that it is the process of deciding where you will allocate your resources. For example, when you start a business and need to determine which business to go into, you are making a corporate strategy decision. Corporate strategy applies to existing businesses, too. In this instance, the strategic decision primarily aims to determine where to allocate resources at an enterprise level. Three main types of corporate strategy decisions are directional, portfolio-related, and what strategy practitioners call parenting. See Table 3.

Directional Strategies

As the name suggests, directional strategies are decisions regarding the overall direction of an enterprise. There are three types of directional strategies: growth, stability, and retrenchment.

Directional Growth Strategies

Growth strategies describe the kind of growth trajectory the firm wishes to pursue. The trajectory can be a concentration on vertical or horizontal growth within existing product lines. By vertical growth, we are referring to backward and forward integration.

Backward integration means taking over the business of suppliers. For example, a bread manufacturer might take over the flour milling business that supplies flour to the bread manufacturer. This would typically be done to secure the sources of raw material supplies or reduce costs.

On the other hand, forward integration is the opposite of backward integration. It refers to the situation where an enterprise takes over the distribution of its products. One motivation for doing this would be to enhance the distribution chain's efficiency to gain a competitive advantage.

Table 3: Key elements of corporate strategy

CORPORATE STRATEGY			
Directional	• Growth	o Concentration	
			– Vertical growth
			– Horizontal growth
		o Diversification	
			– Concentric
			– Conglomerate
	• Stability	o Pause	
		o No change	
		o Profit	
	• Retrenchment	o Turnaround	
		o Captive company	
		o Divestment	
		o Liquidation	
Portfolio Analysis	• BCG Growth Matrix • GE Business screen		
Corporate parenting	• Business units and product lines • Organizational structure		

Horizontal growth, on the other hand, refers to expansion into adjacent product categories or geographies, such as new overseas markets.

There are multiple other ways an enterprise can achieve horizontal growth. These include licensing other manufacturers to produce the enterprise's brands; entering into franchise agreements with third parties to use the enterprise's brand names in exchange for a royalty; entering into joint ventures with other firms; acquiring other firms; setting up new manufacturing facilities in new locations; and outsourcing production to save costs.

Directional Stability Strategies

Another key directional strategy is stability. This refers to when an enterprise makes a conscious strategic decision to halt expansion and consolidate its existing position.

Stability strategy decisions can be grouped into pause, no-change, and profit. Pausing means precisely that: pausing to take stock of things before making the next big strategic move. This decision may be occasioned by a change in the industry or the political situation in the country that may warrant utmost caution in business operations. This is typically a temporary strategy.

Also, a no-change strategy may be necessary when the enterprise believes it has reached a point where further expansion is impractical.

For example, a mining operation where the remaining mineral deposits do not warrant investment in additional extractive capacity.

On the other hand, a profit strategy is a deliberate effort to support profitability by halting new investments or cutting costs. A profit strategy is tempting for an enterprise under intense pressure from its shareholders to show short-term profitability.

Directional Retrenchment Strategies

Retrenchment strategies are usually applied when an enterprise has entered a loss-making mode and wishes to take dramatic action to change course. There are four main retrenchment strategies: turnaround, captive company, divestment, and liquidation.

A turnaround strategy entails taking quick action to stem further losses and implementing operational efficiency measures to save the enterprise. As the name suggests, this strategy may necessitate laying off some staff and changing the organizational structure.

A captive strategy is when the enterprise enters into exclusivity contracts with its suppliers or customers to secure a supply of inputs at pre-determined prices or to secure a revenue stream without incurring marketing costs. In other words, the enterprise becomes captive to its customer or supplier.

A divestment strategy may be a last-resort strategy in which the enterprise decides to exit an industry because it has no realistic prospect of maintaining a competitive position.

Finally, liquidation is a strategy forced upon the enterprise by business circumstances when operating in the industry is no longer tenable. An extreme example is when a company is forced to fold up because of a change in legislation prohibiting its continued operation in a country.

Portfolio Analysis

Portfolio analysis is a way of analyzing business units or product lines based on their relative competitiveness to determine how best to allocate resources, both time and money.

Strategy practitioners use two portfolio analysis methodologies: the BCG (or growth-share) matrix and the GE Business screen. The former is more popular.

The BCG Matrix

Bruce Henderson of the Boston Consulting Group (BCG) developed and published the BCG matrix in 1970. The matrix is a simple and powerful way of analyzing businesses and product lines based on their growth and competitive potential. It groups products into four categories: Cash Cows, Stars, Dogs, and Question Marks (Figure 6).

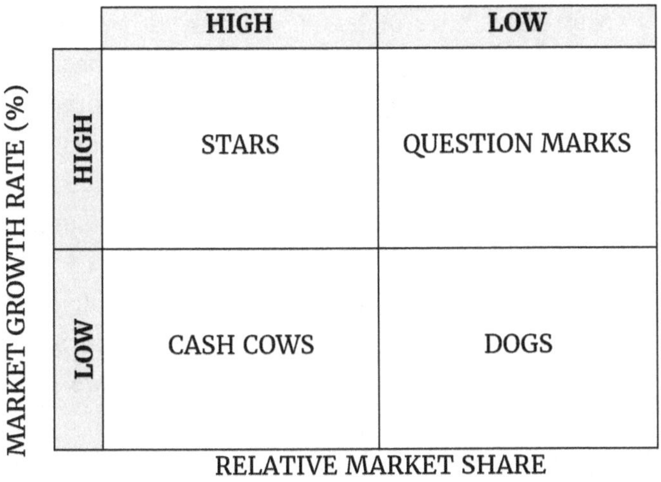

<table>
<tr><td></td><td>HIGH</td><td>LOW</td></tr>
<tr><td>HIGH</td><td>STARS</td><td>QUESTION MARKS</td></tr>
<tr><td>LOW</td><td>CASH COWS</td><td>DOGS</td></tr>
</table>

MARKET GROWTH RATE (%) — vertical axis

RELATIVE MARKET SHARE — horizontal axis

Figure 6: BCG Growth-Share Matrix framework

The term cash cow is common parlance in organizations, although many people may not necessarily use it in strict BCG Growth Matrix terms.[58]

How does one categorize businesses and product lines into these four categories, one might ask? And what do the four categories mean?

The matrix is a 2x2 matrix used primarily to determine where to allocate resources, cash in, and exit. The vertical axis shows the market growth rate, and the horizontal axis shows the relative market share. This results in the matrix shown in Figure 6.

Stars are product lines or business units with relatively high market share in a rapidly growing market. These are typically the enterprise's flagship brands. They require a lot of cash investment to remain competitive, but they can sustain themselves. Over time, when the market growth rate slows down, they become cash cows and generate surplus cash that can be invested to support Question Marks.

Question Marks are typically new products or business units that require a lot of investment to grow into Stars. However, if they do not grow, they could decline into Dogs and be best removed from the portfolio.

As the name suggests, Cash Cows are product lines that have gone beyond the peak of their life cycle and are, therefore, ripe for milking before they decline to become Dogs.

Dogs are products with no potential for growth. The organization should, therefore, abandon them.

A key consideration in using the BCG Matrix in corporate strategy is that the organization should strive for a balanced portfolio. This may necessitate innovating in a few Question Marks, maintaining Stars to support the enterprise's dominance in the market, and some Cash Cows to provide the cash needed for new investments.

There are several underlying assumptions beneath the BCG Matrix that are beyond the scope of this book.

The GE Business Screen

The GE Matrix is a more complicated matrix developed jointly by General Electric and McKinsey & Company consultants in the 1970s. The GE Business Screen has nine quadrants, as depicted in Figure 8. [59]

<table>
<tr><td rowspan="3">INDUSTRY ATTRACTIVENESS</td><td>HIGH</td><td>Winners</td><td>Winners</td><td>Question Marks</td></tr>
<tr><td>MEDIUM</td><td>Winners</td><td>Average</td><td>Losers</td></tr>
<tr><td>LOW</td><td>Profit Producers</td><td>Losers</td><td>Losers</td></tr>
<tr><td></td><td></td><td>STRONG</td><td>AVERAGE</td><td>WEAK</td></tr>
</table>

MARKET STRENGTH/COMPETITIVE POSITION

Figure 7: GE Business Screen

In theory, the GE Business Screen should provide more insights than the BCG Matrix, but it is more complicated to generate.

Parenting Strategy

Parenting strategy relates to an enterprise's choices regarding the best-suited organizational structures to drive the organizational agenda and strategy within the different business units. Also, while portfolio analysis allows the enterprise to determine the most optimal resource allocation, a parenting strategy allows the enterprise to determine the ideal mix of competencies and capabilities. This strategy may necessitate shifting people around the business units to match strategic business needs with the applicable talent required to drive the strategic plan.

BUSINESS STRATEGY

Business strategy is the second level of the strategy framework. It is the core of a distinct business unit's strategy and is aligned with corporate strategy.[60]

Sometimes, people talk about corporate strategy when they are, in fact, referring to business strategy. Business strategies are of two types: competitive and cooperative.

Competitive strategies can be either lower-cost or differentiation strategies. Additionally, lower-cost strategies can be further classified into cost leadership or cost focus strategies, while differentiation strategies can be classified as differentiation or differentiation focus strategies, depending on the broadness or narrowness of the target market.

Table 4: Key elements of business strategy

BUSINESS STRATEGY	
Competitive	Lower cost • Cost leadership • Cost focus
	Differentiation • Differentiation • Differentiation focus
Cooperative	Mutual service consortia
	Joint ventures
	Licensing
	Value chain partnerships

Conversely, cooperative strategies are strategic alliances with other firms. They include mutual service consortia, joint ventures, licensing arrangements, and value chain partnerships.

Competitive Strategies

As earlier pointed out, a business strategy is, in essence, a set of choices that a business makes to offer unique value to its target customers and win in the market where it has chosen to compete. Companies can compete by providing products at a lower cost or differentiating themselves in other ways.

A company that chooses a low-cost strategy deliberately sets prices to outcompete its market rivals. However, such a strategy has a significant disadvantage. It could lead to a price war with the attendant downward spiral in market prices. This could, in turn, mean low profitability for players in that industry. Therefore, price competition should be approached with caution.

A lower-cost strategy focused on a niche market segment is a cost-focused strategy. In this strategy, the company focuses on a particular customer group instead of using a lower-cost strategy for a broad target market. The latter is the cost leadership strategy.

Product differentiation is a more effective competitive strategy that strives to offer unique value to its customers. This can be done in various ways, such as offering free after-sales service, better product packaging than competitors, and a quick turnaround in the supply of the product or service to the customer vis-à-vis competitors. By differentiating this way, the company can charge a premium for the product and still be the customers' preferred product.

A company can decide to pursue a differentiation strategy to only a narrow target group in the market. In this instance, such a strategy is called a differentiation focus strategy.[61]

Cooperative Strategies

As the name suggests, cooperative strategies are based on the recognition that success is dependent on cooperation.

Several factors could necessitate such cooperative strategies, such as legislation, access to markets, access to technologies, production resources, and many others.

Typical cooperative strategies include consortia, joint ventures, licensing agreements, and value chain partnerships.

FUNCTIONAL STRATEGY

Business strategies have to be cascaded downwards in an organization. To this end, good business practice dictates that each functional area in a business unit should prepare a functional strategy aligned with the business unit's strategies.

The typical functional areas for business units are marketing, finance, research and development, operations, human resources, and information systems. Depending on the nature of the business, there could be others.

For example, in the marketing function, functional strategies would cover market development, focusing on improving existing markets to sustain a foothold and strategy designed to enter new markets. Product development strategies would include developing new products for existing and new markets.

Marketing strategies would also include sales promotion campaigns to push products into the market and advertising campaigns to create or accelerate consumer demand (pull) for the company's products.

Table 5: Key elements of functional strategies

FUNCTIONAL STRATEGY	
Marketing	• Market development • Product development • Push strategy • Pull strategy • Skim pricing • Penetration pricing
Finance	• Equity and debt financing • Dividends
R&D	• Technological leader • Technological follower
Operations	• Mass production • Continuous improvement • Mass customization • Modular manufacturing
Human Resources	• Diversity • Temporary workers • 360–degree feedback • Work teams
Information Systems	• Extranets for customer and supplier integration

Marketing strategies may also include skim pricing (pricing at a premium) for new products to capitalize on their novelty or penetration pricing (low pricing) to entrench new products.

Finance strategies could encompass choices regarding debt or equity financing and dividend policy.

Research and Development (R&D) functional strategies are key for many businesses today. Here, the company chooses whether to be a leader and leverage the benefits of being the pioneer or a follower to prevent the potential pitfalls of being first. R&D strategies can include both product and process innovations. Such strategies can be critical in driving an organization's differentiation strategies.

Operations functional strategies can significantly enhance a firm's competitiveness. Operations strategies would include selecting the type of production process used (mass production, job order, mass customization) and continuous improvement strategies.

No organization can achieve success without people. Accordingly, human resources functional strategies are essential. They include choices around the cadre of staff to be hired, performance management, pay structures, training, and development.

Information system functional strategies are becoming increasingly essential for most businesses as the technological landscape becomes more sophisticated.

Information system strategies can create a significant competitive advantage for a firm. For example, integrating customer order placement with the organization's demand fulfillment systems can dramatically impact sales turnover.

The Story of Equity Bank

One of the largest banks in Kenya today is Equity Bank. James Munga founded the company in 1984 as a building society. The building society grew in fits and starts for several years. Competition from other long-established financial institutions was tough. In 1995, the building society was in financial trouble. It had accumulated losses of KShs 33 million, 54% of the loans were non-performing, and the organization's general financial health was dire. Because of this, the institution was on bankruptcy notice from the Central Bank of Kenya. In a nutshell, the bank was on the verge of collapse.

And then something happened in 1995. James Mwangi, a customer of the bank, joined the bank as a manager. Within a short period, he was elevated to the position of managing director.

To cut a long story short, James Mwangi started implementing a turnaround strategy that resulted in the bank's complete transformation.

At the end of 2019, Equity had assets totaling KShs 673.7 billion (US$ 6.7 billion). The Banker's Top 100 African Banks ranked Equity as the seventh-largest bank in Africa.[62]

There are many other success stories of firms that have developed and implemented winning strategies.

CHAPTER 10

Strategic Planning

"Discipline is the bridge between goals and accomplishment."
—Jim Rohn

THE EXTENT TO WHICH SCHOLARS have researched and developed ideas on how to run businesses strategically is mind-boggling. The question that arises is this: If these ideas are so good, why not buy books on strategy and use them in the same way as painting with numbers to ensure business success? The answer to this question is simple: developing and implementing strategies is hard work.

Developing winning strategies requires great energy to gather data, analyze it to generate insights, explore different options, and develop strategies. It requires hard and smart thinking.

Developing Strategies

But where does one start in developing winning strategies? This is probably one of the most challenging but important questions any business leader must contend with: whether or not they have undergone formal strategy training.

If truth be told, there is a lot of fuzziness in the field. Only expensive consultants can bravely claim a firm grip on the best methods of developing winning strategies.

However, it is not all doom and gloom. Over the years, practitioners have developed several processes and tools that can help them develop effective strategies. This chapter will focus on these.

The Strategy Development Process

In most instances, the need for strategy development will be triggered by the timing of a firm's planning cycle or when one joins an existing organization with the specific mandate to develop strategies to steer the organization in a new direction. In either of these situations, one would ultimately need to retrofit the strategy development process to the firm's existing planning cycle in one way or another. To simplify matters, we will explore the strategy-making process within the typical planning framework shown in Figure 8.

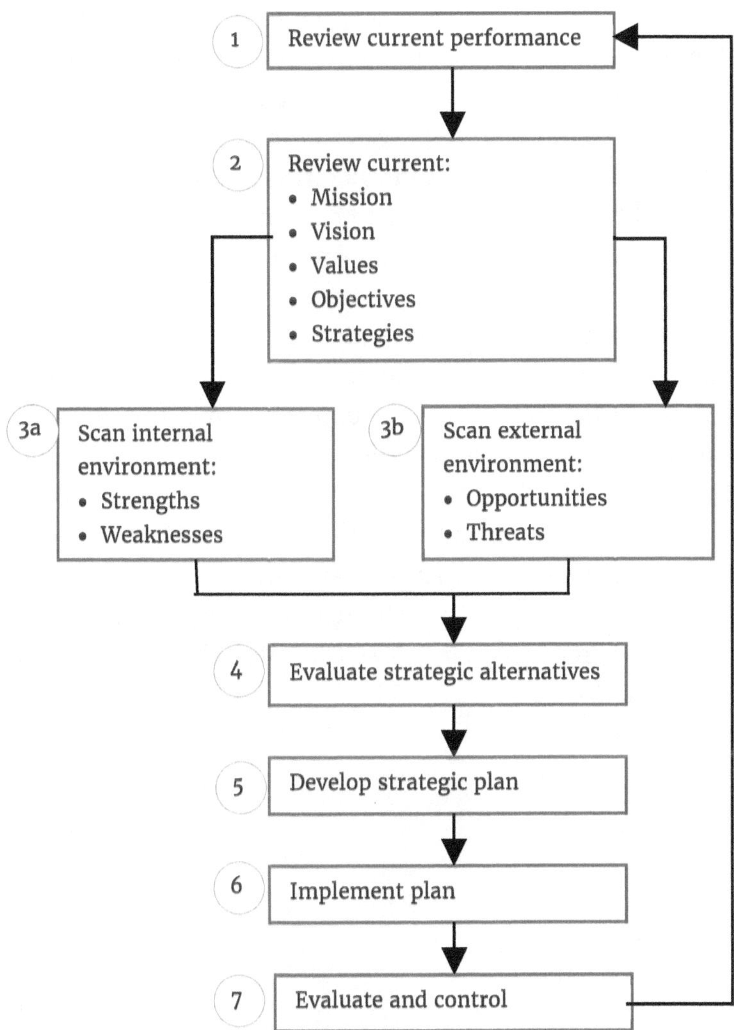

Figure 8: Typical strategic planning cycle

The first step in the strategy development process is to compare actual performance against previous business plans—the more detailed the review process, the better. Comparing actual performance against plans provides valuable insights into the areas that require close attention in the subsequent strategy development process. It also helps in recalibrating the company's long-term goals and objectives. This step would obviously not be necessary for someone developing strategies for a new firm.

One should pay special attention to financial performance. The total of all the implemented strategies and action plans will crystallize into financial outcomes manifested in the company's income statements, cash flows, and balance sheets.

The second important step is to review the firm's vision, mission, objectives, strategies, and policies. But what are these, a non-strategy practitioner might wonder? Table 6 shows the key questions that indicate what these terms represent.

Table 6: Key strategic planning questions

Mission	• What business are we in? • Why do we exist? • Who do we serve? • How do we bring value?
Vision	• Where are we going?
Values	• What do we stand for? • How will we behave? • What do we believe in?
Goals	• What are we trying to achieve?
Objectives	• What concrete deliverables will make the goals come to life?
Strategies	• How are we going to progress to achieve our objectives? • How shall we differentiate ourselves in the marketplace?
Tactics	• What do we need to do?
Action Plans	• How will we do it? • Who will take responsibility for each action? When will they do it?

Mission

The mission is the company's *raison d'être*—that is, the reason for the firm's existence.

You need to ask yourself four questions: What business are we in? Why do we exist? Who do we serve? And how do we bring value? After answering these questions, you should write down a statement that encapsulates all the ideas in a manner that can be understood by everyone who interacts with the organization. It provides clarity on the "who," "what," and "why" of the company.

Below are a few examples of mission statements of some of the most successful companies today.

Amazon: "To be Earth's most customer-centric company, where customers can find and discover anything they might want to buy online, and endeavors to offer its customers the lowest possible prices."

Tesla: "To accelerate the world's transition to sustainable energy."

TED: "Spread ideas."

LinkedIn: "To connect the world's professionals to make them more productive and successful."

*Nike: "Bring inspiration and innovation to every athlete in the world.**
**If you have a body, you are an athlete."*

PayPal: *"To build the web's most convenient, secure, cost-effective payment solution."*[63]

A well-crafted mission statement should contain three key ingredients. Firstly, it should indicate the customers that you will be targeting. Secondly, it should identify your service or product offerings. Thirdly, it should indicate the geography within which you intend to operate.[64,65]

You would want to review the firm's mission jointly with other members of your organization's leadership team. This will ensure buy-in and bring the mission to life for everyone in the organization.

Vision

A vision statement articulates what the firm wants to be in the long term. In other words, how you would want people to see your firm in the distant future. When reviewing the vision, a key question is: where are we going?

Below are a few examples of vision statements.

Amazon: *"Our vision is to be earth's most customer-centric company; to build a place where people can come to find and discover anything they might want to buy online."*

Ikea: *"Our vision is to create a better everyday life for many people."*

<u>*Disney*</u>*: "To entertain, inform and inspire people around the globe through the power of unparalleled storytelling, reflecting the iconic brands, creative minds, and innovative technologies that make ours the world's premier entertainment company."*[66]

A vision statement should ideally be concise. Something people can easily remember and draw inspiration from. A rallying call. It should also have a long-term focus. It should trigger a positive emotion about the firm's future. Also, it should talk about the impact you intend to have in the world. Something that represents your imagination of something that does not exist but that you aspire to accomplish in the future.

A key distinction between the vision and mission is that the vision is something the organization's founder intended to accomplish in the long term. Accordingly, a vision should ideally be something unchangeable in the short term. On the other hand, a mission may be tweaked in the short term, depending on the current business landscape and dynamics. For example, a significant technological shift may necessitate a re-orientation of the firm's mission. In other words, the vision guides the mission.

Values

After reviewing the mission and vision, it is time to review the firm's values. Values describe the standards of behavior expected from everyone within the organization and its stakeholders. In other words, these are the fundamental beliefs you hold dear and that guide conduct by all employees within the organization. The standards that will guide everyone's actions when nobody is looking. The ethical rules of conduct that everyone in the organization will live by. These are the things that should define the culture of the organization.

Below are examples of the values of selected companies.

Microsoft
Our values align to our mission, support our culture, and serve as a declaration of how we treat each other, our customers, and our partners.

Respect
We recognize that the thoughts, feelings, and backgrounds of others are as important as our own.

Integrity
We are honest, ethical, and trustworthy.

Accountability
We accept full responsibility for our decisions, actions, and results.[67]

Equity Bank
Professionalism
Integrity
Creativity & Innovation
Teamwork
Unity of Purpose
Respect & Dignity for Customers
Effective Corporate Governance

The first letters of the seven components of the Equity Bank values form the word PICTURE.[68]

Objectives

Objectives are the concrete, quantifiable aims the company sets out to accomplish within a specific time frame. The criteria generally used to judge the quality of an objective is "SMART," which stands for "Specific, Measurable, Achievable, Realistic, and Time-bound."

Reviewing the objectives set in the preceding planning cycle and developing new objectives during the strategic planning process is important.

Strategies

After gaining clarity on the company's overall direction and setting clear SMART objectives, the next step is to review the status of existing strategies and the underlying initiatives. This review will highlight strategies that have not been fully actualized and need to be retained. It should also reveal strategies that require tweaking in light of the current business dynamics.

This review should set the stage for a full-blown SWOT (Strengths, Weaknesses, Opportunities, Threats) analysis to tease out a complete suite of strategies and strategic initiatives required to achieve the company's revised objectives.

As previously stated, winning strategies are the "hows" of differentiating oneself in the marketplace to achieve the set objectives. A firm can develop several strategies to accomplish each of its objectives.

The development of strategies is both an art and a science. It requires deep thinking, foresight, and intuition. It also requires hard work, which ultimately makes the most significant difference in the organization's success.

This stage of the planning process will typically take the most time. Multiple tools are available to assist practitioners in making strategic decisions. Some people have made careers by helping business people use different strategic planning tools. We will look at some of the tools in the next chapter.

PART V

STRATEGIC PLANNING TOOLS

CHAPTER 11

Tools, Models, and Frameworks

"Someone's sitting in the shade today because someone planted a tree a long time ago."
—Warren Buffet

THE PRECEDING CHAPTERS HAVE PRESENTED several ideas about strategy. However, one of the most overwhelming and probably intimidating aspects of strategy development, especially for a novice, is the number of tools and frameworks used in the strategic planning process.

There are good reasons for the plethora of frameworks and tools. But perhaps the main reason is that all practitioners are continually trying to dig for insights that will help them develop effective strategies in the perpetual quest for enhancing their organizations' performance.

From my experience, those who put in the effort ultimately get better results than those who do not take the task seriously.

Strategic planning tools are like the chisel of a sculptor. When a sculptor looks at a piece of marble, he does not see the oddly shaped natural object from nature; he sees the image of a beautiful figure embedded in the rock. And all he needs to do is chip away at the stone to reveal the beauty. The outcome of such an exercise can sometimes be outstanding, as evidenced by such magnificent sculptures as the "David" sculpture by Michelangelo, currently on display at the Galleria Dell'Accademia in Florence.

We shall look at the strategy tools used in the first two major phases of the strategic planning process described in the preceding chapter, summarized in Figure 9.[69]

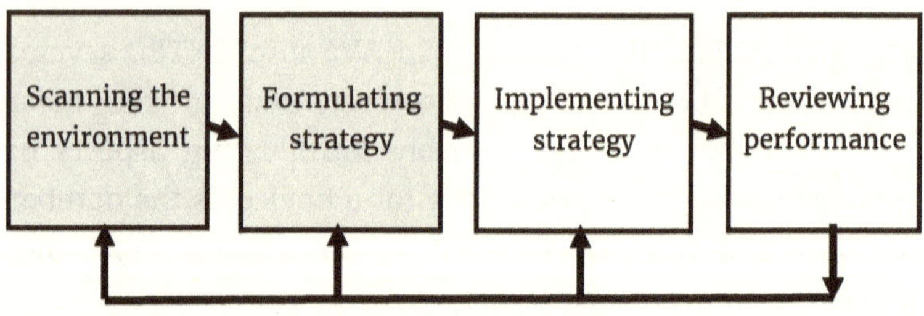

Figure 9: Key phases in strategic planning

* * *

We will examine the most common environmental scanning tools, PEST(EL) and SWOT analysis. We will also examine Scenario and Contingency Planning, which depends heavily on outputs from PESTEL analysis.

We will cover Competitor Analysis, which is crucial in understanding the competitive landscape and an essential ingredient in the strategy development process. We will then look at opportunity sizing, a critical strategic planning tool for most businesses. Finally, we will briefly discuss financial projections.

Multiple other tools and frameworks exist. Readers interested in these can find them in most standard business strategy textbooks or by contacting professional strategy practitioners.

SCANNING THE ENVIRONMENT

Critically scanning the environment to understand the factors that will impact the firm's performance in the future is essential. The scanning process should be performed at two levels, externally and internally.

For a businessman like Akili Mali, scanning the environment is an almost intuitive process he would do daily. However, stepping back and thinking through the environmental factors in a disciplined fashion can add tremendous value and provide insights into refreshing existing strategies or developing new ones.

Over the years, strategy practitioners have developed helpful environmental scanning tools. We will look at some of the most popular and easy-to-use tools: PEST (or PEST(EL) and SWOT analysis.

PEST(EL) ANALYSIS

PEST is a common and relatively easy tool. It is used in environmental scanning using four lenses: "Political, Economic, Social, and Technology," hence the acronym PEST. Some people extend the analysis to the "Environmental and Legal" perspectives to gain a holistic picture of the business environment and its likely effects. When these two perspectives are included, the analysis is called PESTEL.

Scanning the environment from a political perspective includes understanding the government's actions that could impact the business. Examples include national elections and waging war against hostile elements in some parts of the country. The economic perspective includes current and projected interest rates, exchange rates, and other macroeconomic indicators. Interest rates may affect the firm's cost of funds, while exchange rates could affect the cost of imported inputs.

The social perspective includes understanding the changing social dynamics, such as shifts in the demographic profile (age cohorts, mortality rates, and growth rates) and emerging social trends that could affect business.

The technological perspective is a critical look at the technology landscape and how it is likely to positively or negatively affect business. For example, increasing mobile banking technology could affect customers' preferred payment methods for goods and services.

Environmental review is critical in the modern era due to increasing concerns about global warming, water supply sustainability, and the move toward renewable energy.

The legal perspective is essential, too, as it indicates emerging legislative measures that could affect business—for example, potential changes in legislation around ownership of local entities.

Table 7 shows a typical PESTEL analysis with examples of insights and implications for strategic planning.

Table 7: Example of PESTEL Analysis

	Key Trends	Implications
Political	• Political stability gradually set in after general elections earlier in the year	• Renew partnerships with the new administration on key CSR initiatives
Economic	• Rising inflation on the back of a sharp increase in oil prices	• Roll out economy packs to meet consumer demand
Social	• A bulging segment of teens and young adults	• Re-focus the marketing to teens and young adults
Technological	• Increasing reliance on online shopping due to global pandemic	• Enhance the company's online platforms
Environmental	• Environmental lobby pushing for banning of plastic packaging	• Accelerate investment in new paper packaging
Legal	• Parliament reviewing labor laws to increase minimum wages	• Develop a contingency plan for the potential increase in labor costs

SWOT ANALYSIS

After gaining a good understanding of the macro-external factors that could affect the business, the next logical step would be to critically examine the business's internal environment and the immediate external environment (referred to as the task environment) using SWOT analysis, which stands for "Strengths, Weaknesses, Opportunities, and Threats."

SWOT analysis is an excellent brainstorming tool used widely by strategy practitioners in all types of organizations, including non-profit organizations.

SWOT looks at an organization from two angles: internal and external. The internal perspective looks at the "Strengths and Weaknesses" of the organization. In contrast, the external view looks at the "Threats and Opportunities" facing the organization."

A Word of Caution

People can create endless lists of weaknesses and threats. For some reason, the lists of opportunities and strengths are typically much shorter.

Also, there are times when confusion creeps in when an item is classified under more than one category. For example, some people may consider long service in the company a strength and a weakness. It may be a strength because those who have been with the firm for a long time have much experience and knowledge about the business.

On the other hand, it may be a weakness, considering that long-serving employees' knowledge and experience may gradually become redundant due to a fast-changing, technologically-driven business environment.

Another SWOT analysis challenge is determining the weights assigned to the strengths, weaknesses, opportunities, and threats. This challenge can be enormous and is frequently resolved in sub-optimal ways, for example, by the opinion of whoever shouts loudest in the room.

One can use quantitative techniques to address this challenge, such as weighting, rating, and scoring the different factors. However, such an approach can quickly descend into analysis paralysis.

The trick with SWOT is to be down-to-earth and pragmatic. Avoiding being carried away by hyperbole or the loudest voices, in other words, using common sense to determine what matters most for the business is key.

* * *

Turning to the specific example of the Akili Mali Pet Shop, a SWOT analysis may highlight several factors that would inform strategy development during the third year of operation. See Table 8.

Table 8: Sukuma Wiki SWOT analysis

Strengths	Weaknesses
<u>Strengths</u> • Location close to target customers • Highly motivated workforce	<u>Weaknesses</u> • Behind on staff training • Sub-optimal IT infrastructure
<u>Opportunities</u> • Expansion into new up-country malls	<u>Threats</u> • Increasing competition from copycats • New legislation in process that will restrict imports of pet foods

The obvious question from this kind of SWOT analysis is: "So what?"

The answer is to develop strategies for leveraging strengths, minimizing weaknesses, staving off threats, and exploiting opportunities.

In the case of Akili Mali Pet Shop, strategies may include negotiating long-term lease contracts for existing premises and enhancing the IT infrastructure to better serve customers (allowing them to place orders online and enabling the demand forecasting team to plan logistics more effectively). The company could also increase marketing activities to prevent competitors from gaining inroads into the Akili Mali territories.

* * *

Another Word of Caution

While competition might be a significant threat to the business, one should not lose sight of the unique value proposition that Akili Mali offers its target customers. Other players may still come into the market and provide different value to another market segment, thereby helping to spur growth in the pet food business in Nairobi without adversely affecting Akili Mali. Accordingly, Akili Mali should be careful to avoid the temptation of price competition, which could lead to a downward price spiral that could ultimately be detrimental to all players in the industry.

SCENARIO AND CONTINGENCY PLANNING

History of Scenario and Contingency Planning

Scenario and contingency planning have roots in the US military, dating back to the end of World War II. At that time, countries were grappling with the challenges of determining the best weapons systems to develop in preparation for an increasingly uncertain future.

The Rand Corporation, an offshoot of a joint project between the US Air Force and the Douglas Aircraft Company, was the first to develop formal scenario planning techniques. At that time, the Rand Corporation was headed by Herman Khan. The scenario planning project was dubbed "thinking the unthinkable." It was instrumental in the development of early warning systems for the US Air Defense System Missile Command.

Herman Khan later left the Rand Corporation to establish the Hudson Institute. Around that time, scenario planning techniques were declassified. Organizations later adopted the techniques in the public and private sectors.[70]

Shell Oil Company is often cited as an example of an excellent application of scenario planning techniques. The company effectively planned for the 1973 oil crisis.[71]

Gerston Berger, a French philosopher, used scenario planning techniques extensively in the 1950s for long-range planning, focusing on France's political and social landscape.[72]

What is Scenario and Contingency Planning?

Scenario and contingency planning are extensions of PEST(EL) analysis. One of the underlying drivers of scenario and contingency planning is realizing that a single or multiple unexpected catastrophic events can easily destroy an organization. From a strategic standpoint, an organization can wither the vagaries of major adverse events and come out on top of its competitors by careful analysis and planning for plausible multiple alternative futures.[73] An organization can take pre-emptive action rather than merely reacting to events when they occur.[74]

Scenario planning also creates a proactive mindset, critical in today's dynamic and rapidly changing world. Varun and Melon (2009) put it more bluntly: scenario planning helps prevent two typical decision-making errors: over-confidence and tunnel vision. An example will illustrate what Varun and Melon had in mind.

In a conversation between Newton Baker, US Secretary of War, and Brigadier General Billy Mitchell in 1910, the latter described how airplanes could become essential in naval warfare. However, to Newton Barker, such an idea was laughable. He said:

"That idea is so damned nonsensical and impossible that I'm willing to stand on the bridge of a battleship while that nitwit tries to hit it from the air."[75]

Ironically, Scientific American, a prestigious journal, affirmed the War Secretary's views in a publication of the journal in 1910.[76]

The following quotation from Schoemaker (1995) is noteworthy:

When contemplating the future, it is useful to consider three classes of knowledge: (1) things we know we know, (2) things we know we don't know, and (3) things we don't know we don't know.

Various biases – overconfidence, under- and over- prediction, the tendency to look for confirming evidence – plague all three, but the greatest havoc is caused by the third. Although there are no foolproof techniques, focusing attention on two and three can gain much improvement. And this is where scenario planning excels since it is essentially a study of our collective ignorance. It institutionalizes the hunt for weak signals.

Good scenarios challenge tunnel vision by instilling a deeper appreciation for the myriad factors that shape the future. Scenario planning requires intellectual courage to reveal evidence that does not fit our current conceptual maps, especially when it threatens our existence. Nonetheless, what may initially seem to be bleak scenarios could, in fact, hold the seeds of new business and unrecognized opportunity. But those opportunities can only be perceived if you actively look for them. (pp. 38-39).[77]

The reality is that we live in an increasingly uncertain future. The roles of managers and other leaders are becoming increasingly risky and demanding. They are expected to take decisive action to deal with uncertainties when they crystallize. The degree of uncertainty tends to increase the further away on the horizon a manager looks, as illustrated by the Cone of Uncertainty developed by Geldenhuys (2006).[78]

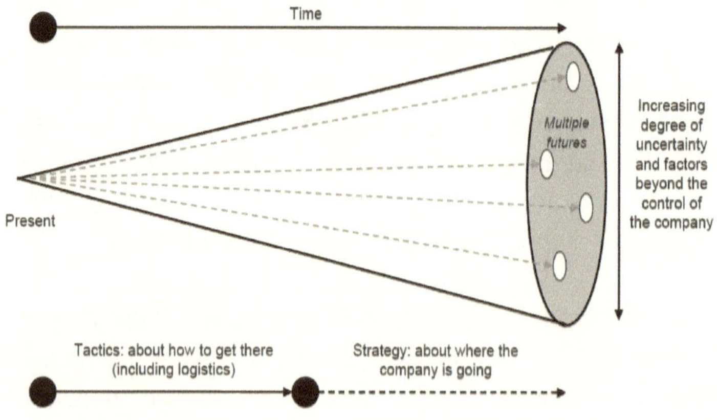

Figure: 10 The Cone of Uncertainty

Uncertainty increases the further away we look in the future. Adapted from "A change navigation-based scenario planning approach: An afro-centric developing country perspective," by C.A. Geldenhuys, 2006, *Doctoral thesis, University of Johannesburg, South Africa,* 37,795–812. Copyright 2006 by Geldenhuys.

Scenario and contingency planning is not about accurately predicting the future. One should think of it as a technique of constructively anticipating alternative futures and translating the uncertainties into plans that can take advantage of the upside potential of the uncertainties or mitigate the likely adverse effects.[79,80]

An Example of UPS

In the late 2000s, fears of a SARS avian flu pandemic created jitters across the globe. UPS, a shipping company, developed scenarios and contingency plans to deal with the potential emergence of the SARS avian flu that could disrupt air traffic and seriously affect the UPS business.

The SARS pandemic did not occur. However, an equally devastating event occurred in 2010, namely, the volcanic eruption at Eyjafjallajökull in Iceland, seriously affecting air transportation. UPS's business was not significantly disrupted because it already had a contingency plan to deal with a similar catastrophe. All it did was activate its contingency plan for SARS. Their competitors, without scenario and contingency planning, were not so lucky.[81]

Different Scenario and Contingency Planning Methods

Over the years, practitioners have developed different scenario and contingency planning methods. Bradfield (2005) describes it as "methodological chaos.[82]

We will not dwell on this minefield. Instead, we will focus on a straightforward approach that should yield the desired results.

This approach has five steps: scanning the environment to identify significant events that may impact the business (positively or negatively); prioritizing the events on their likelihood of occurrence, the speed at which they could occur, and the magnitude of their potential impact on the business; selecting the few most plausible scenarios and developing narratives about potential alternative futures relating to those scenarios; determining the key indicators that will serve as warnings of the onset of the events; and developing contingency plans that will be quickly activated to deal with the events (including allocation of resources).[83]

The key is to keep things simple, focus on the potential impact of events on the business, and take realistic actions to deal effectively with them. Figure 12 shows a simple job aid that can be used in the scenario and contingency planning process.

Priority Event				
Narrative of likely scenario				
Strategies for addressing the event				
Contingency Plan	Action	Person Responsible	Others involved	Resources Required
Triggers for Action				
Stakeholder Engagement Plan				

Figure 11: Scenario and Contingency Planning Job Aid

COMPETITOR ANALYSIS

As discussed in detail in the preceding chapters, a key aim of strategy is to gain leverage over competitors. Therefore, we need to understand our competitors well in order to develop effective strategies. As Sun Tzu once said:

"If you know the enemy and know yourself, you need not fear the result of a hundred battles. If you know yourself but not the enemy, for every victory gained you will also suffer a defeat. If you know neither the enemy nor yourself, you will succumb in every battle."

The techniques of analyzing competition range from the simple anecdotal analysis of the competitive landscape that can be done on the back of an envelope to sophisticated data-driven analysis. The latter is preferable as it is more insightful.

* * *

The first thing you would want to know is the share of the market that your competitors control. Such an insight would help determine the kind of strategies to deploy. For example, if you realize you are the market leader, you may need to ensure that you remain on top by using all means possible.

That could necessitate enhancing your brand image through advertising and entering into exclusivity contracts with your customers (if legally permissible).

If, on the other hand, you discover that you are a minor player amongst a multitude of other players, then you may decide to explore alternative niches where you can distinguish yourself and gain a foothold.

The market share described above is perhaps one of today's most common strategic analysis tools.

But you can go one step further to gain even more meaningful insights. For example, if you are in the fast-moving consumer goods business (FMCG), you can analyze market share by consumer groups such as teens, tweens, young adults, adults, and others. You can also cut up the data by geography. In the process, you could discover the existence of significantly underserved markets that are ready for your taking. You could also view the data from a "day-part" perspective, e.g., early morning, mid-morning, lunchtime, etc.

There are multiple other ways you could analyze data to obtain valuable insights. It all depends on the nature of your business, your level of interest, and the kind of analysis you can afford.

* * *

But there is another even more robust way of analyzing your competitors, especially when a few significant players dominate the market.

It entails analyzing your main competitor(s) in great detail, preferably using a cross-functional multidisciplinary project team.

It involves doing thorough research on all aspects of the competitors' business, including the macroeconomic environment in which they operate, their product portfolios, the production facilities they use and their capacities, their suppliers of inputs, their customer base, their pricing policy, the composition of their leadership, their workforce and their competency levels, their route-to-market architecture, and any other aspects of their business that you can think of.

After gathering all that information, the project team should put themselves in the competitors' shoes and develop competitor strategic plans. The hypothetical strategic plans of the competitors would then form the basis for developing robust pre-emptive competitive strategies.

The company will, in effect, be able to predict with a fair amount of accuracy the moves the competitor is likely to make and determine the actions required to quickly and effectively react to such moves.

OPPORTUNITY SIZING

Opportunity Sizing is a powerful method of digging into potential opportunities. The methods used for this purpose are as diverse as there are strategy practitioners. If you wanted to segment strategy practitioners by their level of strategy acumen, an excellent way would be to look at their methods and approaches for opportunity identification and sizing.

It All Starts with Data

While intuition and other subjective considerations are helpful in opportunity identification and sizing, nothing is more powerful than data. Data is the oxygen and blood of opportunity identification and sizing. We can bring this to life by looking at an example of a fast-moving consumer goods industry (e.g., confectionaries, wines, fruit juices, and the like).

Detailed data is gathered about the consumption of products within the industry in which the company operates. The consumption (or sales) data should be sliced and diced into as many categories as possible.

For example, by product category, brand, package type, package size, channel, consumption occasion (at home, away from home, mealtimes, leisure, relaxing, watching TV, on-premise, on-the-go, traveling, working, studying, hanging out), price point, consumer demographic (10-20-year-olds, 30-40-year-olds, 40-50-year-olds, above 50), gender, brand preference indicator, consumption frequency (daily, weekly, monthly), trial and retention drivers, period (day, week, month, year), or other relevant variables.

The data should also be collected for the industry and by competitors.

Other non-industry-specific data should also be added to the mix. This would include historical weather data (temperature, rainfall) and macroeconomic data (interest rates, inflation rates, currency exchange rates).

The analysis of the data set would require the use of a tool such as Excel. Many companies use other custom-built tools.

Triangulating the data in different ways makes it possible to see trends and correlations, revealing various nuggets of opportunities.

Below is a simple hypothetical Opportunity Map that can be generated from such a rich mine of data (Table 8). In this example, sales volume data for 2020 is presented by category for the company and the total industry.

Table 9: 2020 Volume share by category (in standardized units)

Category	Industry	% of Category	Company	% of Category	Market Share
Aaaa	1,800	51%	1,400	70%	78%
Bbbb	700	20%	600	30%	86%
Cccc	400	11%	10	0%	3%
Dddd	600	17%		0%	0%
Total	3,500	100%	2,010	100%	57%

The analysis reveals that the company dominates in the Aaaa and Bbbb product categories, with 78% and 86% market shares, respectively. At the other extreme, the company has a minimal presence in the Cccc and Dddd categories. This may suggest that the company needs to pursue strategies focusing on the first two categories and ignore the last two categories. However, this first set of numbers may not be enough to make such a determination. That is because the numbers reflect market share based only on sales volume.

It would be interesting to go one step further and see what the picture looks like when the sales numbers are converted to revenues (i.e., sales volumes multiplied by selling prices). Table 10 presents a hypothetical Opportunity Map based on revenues.

Table 10: 2020 Market share by revenue (in KShs M)

Category	Industry	% of Category	Company	% of Category	Market Share
Aaaa	1,980	18%	1,540	67%	78%
Bbbb	840	8%	720	31%	86%
Cccc	2,000	18%	50	2%	3%
Dddd	6,000	55%	0	0%	0%
Total	10,820	100%	2,310	100%	21%

By performing the second analysis, the company will realize that although it dominates the market in the first two categories, it represents only 26% percent of industry revenues (i.e., 18% + 8%). The highest industry revenues are in the Cccc and Dccc categories (i.e., 18% + 55%).

In other words, the company is like a shark swimming in ocean waters full of mackerel and bragging about its dominance in that arena without realizing that there are bigger and more sumptuous fish in the same ocean near the estuaries. That revelation would be enough to make the shark of a company blush or move swiftly into the estuaries.

A graphical presentation of the data also makes it easier to spot opportunities. For example, look at the charts presented below (Figures 13 and 20).

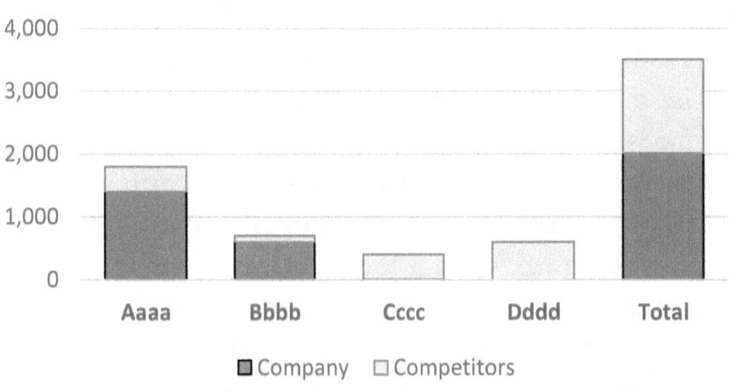

Figure 12: Industry volume by category (SU)

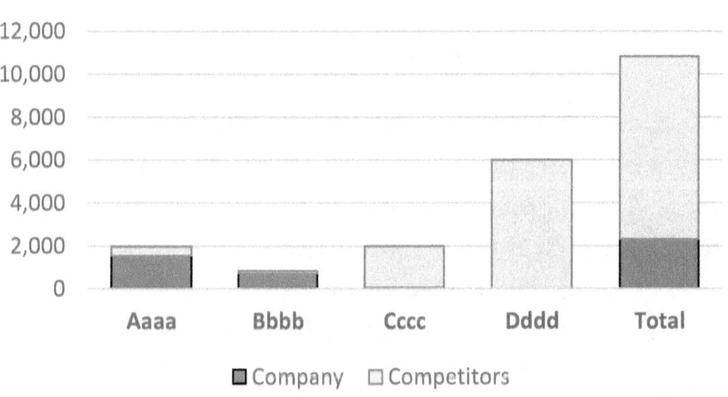

Figure 13: Industry revenues by category (KShs M)

The charts reflect the company's and competitors' share of industry volume and revenues, as shown in Tables 9 and 10. The misalignment between the company's volume and revenue is now vividly clear.

The insights in this hypothetical scenario may not necessarily mean the company is missing out on some big action. It may turn out that the production of Cccc and Dddd products may require exceptionally expensive state-of-the-art equipment beyond the company's means. Therefore, the insight may only confirm the pain and agony of being less endowed with resources than others.

But in the strategy-making world, things should not end there either. The company can glean more insights from the data by looking at many other permutations. For example, by looking at the data by geographical location, the company could discover new markets for the taking.

The company may want to explore other permutations, such as sales by category and consumption occasion, sales by channel and demographic profile, or sales by demographic profile and need state. Indeed, the permutations are almost endless. The thoroughness of the strategy practitioner may determine which is most appropriate.

It is of equal importance to triangulate the data with other factors that are not easily quantifiable and may have emerged from the PESTEL and SWOT analysis. For example, impending legislation could affect the distribution channels, availability of certain inputs, long lead times for obtaining government approvals of new product innovations, and existing inventories of slow-moving products.

Suffice it to say that the more in-depth and more extensive the analysis, the greater the chances of identifying and mapping opportunities, and the more laser-focused and high-quality the company's strategies.

FINANCIAL PROJECTIONS

To conclude our discussion of strategy development, we should not lose sight of our basic economic model. After all, what good is a strategy if it does not add value to our business or lives?

With this in mind, developing projections crystallizing the expected monetary outcomes of implementing our strategies is essential. For commercial enterprises, the strategic plan's final output must be a set of financial projections for the period covered by the strategic plan.

If the projections do not reflect the desired results, we must return to our strategies and tweak them appropriately. This review and refinement is an iterative process and must be done until we end up with a strategic plan that hangs together. One should not be shy about running three, five, ten, fifteen, twenty, or even more iterations. This is a critical step. It ensures the strategic plan is as realistic as possible and provides a firm foundation for future strategy implementation and tracking.

A Final Word

As Sir Winston Churchill once said: "However beautiful the strategy, you should occasionally look at the results."[84]

PART VI

CHOICES HAVE CONSEQUENCES

CHAPTER 12

A New Chapter in Life

"We all make choices, but in the end, our choices make us."
— Ken Levine

THE OUTCOMES OF LIFE ARE shaped by the decisions we make earlier in our lives. Most of the decisions are strategic decisions. With that in mind, it would be interesting to learn what came of Sukuma Wiki and Akili Mali.

SUKUMA WIKI

Sukuma Wiki's return to the veterinary medicine profession was not as smooth as he had anticipated. This had nothing to do with the Sasumua Clinic. It had much to do with the ghosts of his former business enterprise at Kawangware.

Although he had sold the business for a decent sum, he could not pass on his debts to Akili Mali. He had borrowed some money from a local microfinance bank in his name. He had inadvertently forgotten to borrow it in the company's name – a huge strategic blunder. So, of the KShs 2.0 million he received from Akili Mali, he used KShs 1 million to clear the outstanding loan, including the accrued interest and penalties.

So, when he rejoined Sasumua Clinic, Sukuma Wiki only had KShs 350,000 in his possession. The amount would have been considerably more had it not been for his spending spree after selling the business.

The KShs 350,000 was not enough to buy a car, which he required for traveling to and from work. Therefore, he was forced to obtain another loan to cover the cost of a vehicle.

He was already starting in the red as a veterinary doctor.

It took Sukuma Wiki two years to lighten his financial burdens.

* * *

Sukuma Wiki spent the next ten years engrossed in his job as a veterinary doctor. He saved enough money to buy a plot at Mlolongo, on the outskirts of Nairobi. He spent the next two years building a pleasant family home. It was nothing unusual - just a suitable place to accommodate his family, with a sizeable garden for playing with his dogs, Josto and Rasta.

Sukuma Wiki had learned the lessons of frugality the hard way. Memories of the ostentatious outings with Anita were painful reminders of his financial mismanagement as a young man – something that had almost ruined him. But what was more painful was the loss of the pet food business, which he had initially hoped would grow into a large enterprise and make him a wealthy man. The memories were bitter. They were embedded in the dark recesses of his mind, but there was nothing he could do about it.

Around the 21st anniversary of his employment with Sasumua Veterinary Clinic, Sukuma Wiki started imbibing a little wine in the evenings, after meals. It was an easy way of forgetting the past and enjoying momentary bliss.

He particularly enjoyed South African wine. He would talk for hours about the different types of wine from South Africa and other parts of the world.

He would take only one glass a day. After a few months, a single glass was not enough. He increased the servings to two drinks, then to three. But he had a refined taste for wines, and the beverage was draining his finances. Accordingly, he decided to switch to beer.

He would take one cold beer after dinner and feel thoroughly entertained. And just as in the case of wine, one beer gradually became two. And when he reached three bottles, he started getting irritated by the bloating feeling he began to experience. Accordingly, he switched to whiskey.

By his 30th anniversary as an employee of Sasumua Clinic, Sukuma Wiki had become an alcoholic. It was not a wonder that he lost his job later that year.

Sukuma Wiki retired at his home in Mlolongo. He rarely socialized with his friends. He spent most of his waking time in local bars.

Anita had tried endlessly to talk to Sukuma Wiki about his drinking problem to no avail. Interventions by family and friends had also failed. Eventually, Anita decided to call it quits. She could not tolerate it. She filed for a divorce and left to pursue a new independent life.

Today, Sukuma Wiki lives like a recluse – without family or friends - only his two dogs and a cat.

AKILI MALI

The fifteen years of the Akili Mali enterprise were immensely eventful. The business grew much faster than he had anticipated.

But strangely enough, the single thing that seemed to give Akili Mali the greatest sense of satisfaction was not the business's profitability. It was the realization that he was the sole provider of the livelihoods of more than fifty families. This realization had made him particularly sensitive to employee welfare. Indeed, employees were at the core of Akili Mali Enterprise Holdings' growth agenda, the parent company of the three business entities that Akili Mali had created for his business.

His pet food shops had grown significantly in Nairobi. They were present in all the high-end malls in Nairobi and the upcountry. Akili Mali had created Akili Mali Limited as the umbrella entity for all the pet food shops.

He also adopted a backward integration strategy to secure his supplies of high-quality pet foods. Accordingly, he developed a greenfield facility for the manufacture of high-quality pet foods. A global pet foods manufacturer based in Germany awarded him a franchise.

Akili Mali also entered into alliances with overseas manufacturers of certain specialty foods in demand by horse breeders. The margins on the horse food were excellent, helping him generate sufficient cash flows to sustain the pet food manufacturing business after its inception.

The manufacturing business and the strategic alliances came under the umbrella of Akili Products Limited.

One significant benefit of venturing into manufacturing was opening up different packaging options for pet food under the Akili brand name. Because Akili Mali was a stickler for quality, he made inroads into most of the high-end categories and sold his products at a significant premium.

To further improve his operating effectiveness and optimize his costs, Akili Mali set up a business services firm called Akili Mali Management Services Limited. This company provided all the IT and financial services the Akili Mali group required. Akili Mali leased out the extra capacity to other entities in the country.

Because of the organization's increasing complexity, it hired highly qualified functional leaders. Still, he remained the Group CEO to oversee the enterprise at the Group level. However, as part of his succession plan, he recruited a Chief Operating Officer who would eventually take over from him.

Akili Mali's son and daughter joined the company and held senior positions in the Group's Legal and Procurement departments. He transferred to them a 15% equity interest in the enterprise. Akili Mali and his wife, Sophia, retained 85% of the equity interest.

Akili Mali had configured his business so that after the twentieth year, he could afford to go on vacation without worrying about the day-to-day running of the firm.

As he approached the 30th anniversary of Akili Mali Enterprises' creation, he relinquished the company's day-to-day running to his successor, Alif Kasuku. Akili Mali remained Chairman of the Company. He only attended the quarterly Board meetings and the occasional meeting when crucial decisions required his direct input.

* * *

Akili Mali later retired to the beautiful resort town of Ukunda on the south coast of Kenya. He built a big mansion near a golf course, enabling him to indulge in his favorite pastime—golf.

He had become an avid bird watcher and occasionally went on bird hunting safaris in different parts of the country and sometimes out of the country.

One of his crowning achievements was being awarded by the country's president the accolade Chief of the Order of the Golden Heart of Kenya (C.G.H.). The award recognized his immense contribution to the country's welfare through his philanthropic initiatives and the creation of employment opportunities for hundreds of Kenyans through his Akili Mali Enterprises business empire.

Akili Mali epitomized what it means to develop a strategic mindset.

BIBLIOGRAPHY

"How to Write Your Mission Statement." Entrepreneur, October 30, 2003. https://www.entrepreneur.com/article/65230

"In Our Time: Clausewitz and On War." Clark's History Reels. BBC Radio 4, May 20, 2018. https://www.youtube.com/watch?v=2jc5dIzKQpE.

"Top 10 Highest Paid Stars In Kenya Premier League." Youth Village Kenya. Accessed February 7, 2021. https://youthvillage.co.ke/top-10-highest-paid-stars-in-kenya-premier-league/

"Top 5 Highest Paid Footballer in Real Madrid." Great In Sports. G&S, September 12, 2019. https://greatinsports.com/top5/top-5-highest-paid-footballer-in-real-madrid/

Adopted from Hunger, J. D., & Wheelen, T. L. (2014). *Essentials of strategic management* (4th ed.). Upper Saddle River, NJ: Pearson

Allison, G. T. (2018, September). Is war between China and the US inevitable? Retrieved January 15, 2021, from https://www.ted.com/talks/graham_allison_is_war_between_china_and_the_us_inevitable

Allison, G. T. (2018, September). Is war between China and the US inevitable? Retrieved January 15, 2021, from https://www.ted.com/talks/graham_allison_is_war_between_china_and_the_us_inevitable

Arriaga, Alexander F., David L. Hepner, and Angela M. Bader. "'However Beautiful the Strategy, You Should

Occasionally Look at the Results.'" *Anesthesia & Analgesia* 126, no. 1 (2018): 16–18. https://doi.org/10.1213/ane.0000000000002492

Banker, The. "The Banker's Top 100 African Banks 2020." The Banker - Unrivalled coverage of global finance & banking -, 2020. https://www.thebanker.com/Banker-Data/Banker-Rankings/The-Banker-s-Top-100-African-Banks-2020?ct=true.

BCG Matrix (Growth-Share Matrix) EXPLAINED. Business To You, 2020. https://www.youtube.com/watch?v=gNR49lk5dS0&ab_channel=BusinessToYou

Barney, Jay. "Firm Resources and Sustained Competitive Advantage." *Journal of Management* 17, no. 1 (1991): 99–120. https://doi.org/10.1177/014920639101700108

Bradfield, R., Wright, G, Burt, G., Cairns, G, & Van der Heijen, K. (2005). The origins and evolution of scenario techniques in long range business planning. *Futures*, 37,795-812. doi:10.1016/j.futures.2005.01.003

Bradfield, Ron, George Wright, George Burt, George Cairns, and Kees Van Der Heijden. "The Origins and Evolution of Scenario Techniques in Long Range Business Planning." *Futures* 37, no. 8 (2005): 795–812. https://doi.org/10.1016/j.futures.2005.01.003

Byrne, John A. "How to Calculate the Cost of a Harvard MBA." Poets&Quants. MBA Watch, August 11, 2017. https://poetsandquants.com/2017/08/11/what-a-harvard-mba-now-costs/?pq-ab-2=b

Chen, J. (2020, August 28). Nash Equilibrium. Retrieved January 22, 2021, from https://www.investopedia.com/terms/n/nash-equilibrium.asp#:~:text=The%20prisoner's%20dilemma%20is%20a,of%20communicating%20with%20the%20other.&text=The%20Nash%20equilibrium%20in%20this,players%20to%20betray%20each%20other.

Clausewitz, Carl von, Michael Howard, and Peter Paret. Essay. In *On War*, 75. Princeton, NJ: Princeton University Press, 1989

Coonradt, John E. "The Visionary and the Reactionary." Mackinac Center for Public Policy, March 24, 2005. https://www.mackinac.org/7012

Currie-Knight, K. (219, December 17). Finite and Infinite Games (Carse) Explained. Retrieved January 23, 2021, from https://www.youtube.com/watch?v=pODt-jnJfRA&t=14s&ab_channel=KevinCurrie-Knight

Engelhardt, L. M. (Director). (2016, August 9). *Game Theory* [Video file]. Retrieved January 21, 2021, from https://www.youtube.com/watch?v=Ldn34TxmGKE&t=1637s&ab_channel=misesmedia

Entrepreneur Staff. "Mission Statement Definition – Entrepreneur Small Business Encyclopedia." Entrepreneur. Accessed February 5, 2021. https://www.entrepreneur.com/encyclopedia/mission-statement

Geldenhuys, C A. A change navigation-based scenario planning process: an afrocentric, developing country perspective., September 1, 2006. https://ujcontent.uj.ac.za/vital/access/manager/Repository/uj:8547

Green, H. (Director). (2016, September 30). *Game Theory: The Science of Decision-Making* [Video file]. Retrieved January 21, 2021, from https://www.youtube.com/watch?v=MHS-htjGgSY&ab_channel=SciShow

Goldstein, David. "Who Moves The Coffee Markets? Meet The World's Largest Green Coffee Traders." Commodity Trading Guru, January 21, 2021. https://commoditytrading.guru/commodities/who-moves-the-coffee-markets-meet-the-worlds-largest-green-coffee-traders/.

Helis, Jim. "USAWC Expert Discusses Clausewitz." YouTube. USArmyWarCollege, September 6, 2011. https://www.youtube.com/watch?v=pSF_UtEWnCg

History.com Editors, History.com Editors. "Sun Tzu." History.com. A&E Television Networks, November 12, 2009. https://www.history.com/topics/ancient-china/sun-tzu.

Howard, Ron. 2001. **A Beautiful Mind.** United States: Universal Pictures.

Hunger, J. David, and Thomas L. Wheelen. *Essentials of Strategic Management*. Essex: Pearson, 2014

Mark, Joshua J. "Sun-Tzu." Ancient History Encyclopedia. Ancient History Encyclopedia, November 3, 2020. https://www.ancient.eu/Sun-Tzu/.

Matthews, Dylan. "This Is the Best Letter of Recommendation Ever." Vox. Vox, June 6, 2015. https://www.vox.com/2015/6/6/8738229/john-nash-recommendation-letter

Matthews, Dylan. "This Is the Best Letter of Recommendation Ever." Vox. Vox, June 6, 2015. https://www.vox.com/2015/6/6/8738229/john-nash-recommendation-letter

Microsoft. "Our Corporate Values." About People. Accessed February 5, 2021. https://www.microsoft.com/en-us/about/corporate-values

Miller-Wilson, Kate. "Best Examples of Strong Company Vision Statements." Example Articles & Resources. Accessed February 3, 2021. https://examples.yourdictionary.com/best-examples-of-a-vision-statement.html

Nasar, Sylvia. *A Beautiful Mind*. London: Faber & Faber, 2012

Nash, John F. "Non-Cooperative Games." Dissertation, 1950

Nelson, Erin. "Best Mission Statements: 12 Examples You Need to See." Fond, February 13, 2020. https://www.fond.co/blog/best-mission-statements/

Peterson, G.D., Cumming, G.S. & Carpenter, SR (2003). Scenario planning: a tool for conservation in an uncertain world. *Conservation Biology*, 17 (2), 358-366. Retrieved from http://www.cakex.org/virtual-library/3420

Porter, M. E. (2004). *Competitive strategy*. New York, NY: Free

Porter, Michael E. "How Competitive Forces Shape Strategy." Harvard Business Review, May 20, 2015. https://hbr.org/1979/03/how-competitive-forces-shape-strategy

Porter, Michael E. "How Competitive Forces Shape Strategy." Harvard Business Review, May 20, 2015. https://hbr.org/1979/03/how-competitive-forces-shape-strategy

Porter, Michael E. "What Is Strategy?" Harvard Business Review, November 7, 2019. https://hbr.org/1996/11/what-is-strategy.

Publication. *Equity Group Holdings Plc and Subsidiaries Integrated Report & Financial Statements 2018*. Nairobi, Kenya: Equity Holdings Group PLC, 2019

Schoemaker, P J.H. "Scenario Planning: A Tool for Strategic Thinking Paul J. H. Schoemaker, Sloan Management Review (Winter 1995), Pp. 25–40." *Journal of Product Innovation Management* 12, no. 4 (1995): 355–56. https://doi.org/10.1016/0737-6782(95)97416-s

Schoemaker, Paul J.H. "Scenario Planning: a Tool for Strategic Thinking." *Long Range Planning* 28, no. 3 (1995): 117. https://doi.org/10.1016/0024-6301(95)91604-0

Schoemaker, Paul J. "Forecasting and Scenario Planning: The Challenges of Uncertainty and Complexity." *Blackwell Handbook of Judgment and Decision Making*, 2004, 274–96. https://doi.org/10.1002/9780470752937.ch14

Schwartz, P. (2011, November 8th). Getting ahead of the curve. *Global Business Network.* Retrieved from http://www.gbn.com/ideas/scenarios.php

Sinek, S. (Director). (2016, November 8). *What game theory teaches us about war* [Video file]. Retrieved January 25, 2021, from https://www.youtube.com/watch?v=0bFs6ZiynSU&ab _channel=TEDArchive

Smith, A. (1902). *The wealth of nations* (p. 160). New York: American Home Library

Sonnenschein, H. F. (Director). (2015, December 1). *Game Theory and Negotiation* [Video file]. Retrieved January 21, 2021, from https://www.youtube.com/watch?v=E1ifAXKDyoI&t=5 80s&ab_channel=BeckerFriedmanInstituteatUChicago -BFI

Stauffer, D. (2002). Five reasons why you still need scenario planning. *Harvard Management Update*, Article Reprint No. U0206A, 3-5. Retrieved from http://hbr.org/product/five-reasons-why-you-still- need-scenario-planning/an/U0206A-PDF-ENG

Sunzi, Ralph D. Sawyer, Mei-chun Sawyer, Bin Sun, and Sunzi. 1996. *The complete art of war*. Boulder, Colo: Westview Press.

Thucydides - Another Father of History? - The Peloponnesian War, Thucydides' Trap & Pericles Speech [Video file]. (2019, January 20). Retrieved January 15, 2021, from https://www.youtube.com/watch?v=hYJyApvxr7U&ab _channel=SandRhomanHistory

Thucydides, Crawley, R., & Feetham, R. (1903). *Thucydides' Peloponnesian war*. London, UK: J.M. Dent and.

Turner, N. (2008). Future-proofing your organization. *CEO Journal*, 1-3. Retrieved from http://www.gbn.com/articles/pdfs/GBN_Futureproofi ng.CEO%20j.pdf

Tzu, Sun, Ralph D. Sawyer, and Mei-chn Sawyer. *The Art of War:* Boulder, CO: Westview Press, 1994.

Wulf, T., Meissner, P & Stubner, S. (2010). *A scenario-based approach to strategic planning – Integrating planning and process perspective of strategy.* (Working Paper 1/2010, HHL – Leipzig Graduate School of Management, Center for Scenario Planning – Roland Berger Research Unit, Leipzig, Germany)

"Equity Ranks Position 7 in the List of Top 10 Banks in Africa in The Banker's Top 100 African Banks 2020." Equity Group Holdings, 2020. https://equitygroupholdings.com/equity-ranks-position-7-in-the-list-of-top-10-banks-in-africa-in-the-bankers-top-100-african-banks-2020/

NOTES

1 Porter, Michael E. "What Is Strategy?" Harvard Business Review, November 7, 2019. https://hbr.org/1996/11/what-is-strategy.

2 Porter, M. E. (2004). *Competitive strategy*. New York, NY: Free.

3 Tzu, Sun, Ralph D. Sawyer, and Mei-chn Sawyer. *The Art of War:* Boulder, CO: Westview Press, 1994.

4 Mark, Joshua J. "Sun-Tzu." Ancient History Encyclopedia. Ancient History Encyclopedia, November 3, 2020. https://www.ancient.eu/Sun-Tzu/.

5 History.com Editors, History.com Editors. "Sun Tzu." History.com. A&E Television Networks, November 12, 2009. https://www.history.com/topics/ancient-china/sun-tzu.

6 Mark, Joshua J. "Sun-Tzu." Ancient History Encyclopedia. Ancient History Encyclopedia, November 3, 2020. https://www.ancient.eu/Sun-Tzu/.

7 Mark, Joshua J. "Sun-Tzu." Ancient History Encyclopedia. Ancient History Encyclopedia, November 3, 2020. https://www.ancient.eu/Sun-Tzu/.

8 Tzu, Sun, Ralph D. Sawyer, and Mei-chn Sawyer. *The Art of War:* Boulder, CO: Westview Press, 1994.

9 Sunzi, Ralph D. Sawyer, Mei-chun Sawyer, Bin Sun, and Sunzi. 1996. *The complete art of war*. Boulder, Colo: Westview Press.

10 Sunzi, Ralph D. Sawyer, Mei-chun Sawyer, Bin Sun, and Sunzi. 1996. *The complete art of war*. Boulder, Colo: Westview Press.

---

[11] Sunzi, Ralph D. Sawyer, Mei-chün Sawyer, Bin Sun, and Sunzi. 1996. *The complete art of war.* Boulder, Colo: Westview Press.

[12] "In Our Time: Clausewitz and On War." Clark's History Reels. BBC Radio 4, May 20, 2018. https://www.youtube.com/watch?v=2jc5dIzKQpE.

[13] "In Our Time: Clausewitz and On War." Clark's History Reels. BBC Radio 4, May 20, 2018. https://www.youtube.com/watch?v=2jc5dIzKQpE.

[14] "In Our Time: Clausewitz and On War." Clark's History Reels. BBC Radio 4, May 20, 2018. https://www.youtube.com/watch?v=2jc5dIzKQpE.

[15] "In Our Time: Clausewitz and On War." Clark's History Reels. BBC Radio 4, May 20, 2018. https://www.youtube.com/watch?v=2jc5dIzKQpE.

[16] "In Our Time: Clausewitz and On War." Clark's History Reels. BBC Radio 4, May 20, 2018. https://www.youtube.com/watch?v=2jc5dIzKQpE.

[17] Helis, Jim. "USAWC Expert Discusses Clausewitz." YouTube. USArmyWarCollege, September 6, 2011. https://www.youtube.com/watch?v=pSF_UtEWnCg

[18] "In Our Time: Clausewitz and On War." Clark's History Reels. BBC Radio 4, May 20, 2018. https://www.youtube.com/watch?v=2jc5dIzKQpE.

[19] "In Our Time: Clausewitz and On War." Clark's History Reels. BBC Radio 4, May 20, 2018. https://www.youtube.com/watch?v=2jc5dIzKQpE.

[20] "In Our Time: Clausewitz and On War." Clark's History Reels. BBC Radio 4, May 20, 2018. https://www.youtube.com/watch?v=2jc5dIzKQpE.

[21] Clausewitz, Carl von, Michael Howard, and Peter Paret. Essay. In *On War*, 75. Princeton, NJ: Princeton University Press, 1989

[22] Clausewitz, Carl von, Michael Howard, and Peter Paret. Essay. In *On War*, 75. Princeton, NJ: Princeton University Press, 1989

---

23 "In Our Time: Clausewitz and On War." Clark's History Reels. BBC Radio 4, May 20, 2018. https://www.youtube.com/watch?v=2jc5dIzKQpE.

24 Allison, G. T. (2018, September). Is war between China and the US inevitable? Retrieved January 15, 2021, from https://www.ted.com/talks/graham_allison_is_war_between_china_and_the_us_inevitable

25 Allison, G. T. (2018, September). Is war between China and the US inevitable? Retrieved January 15, 2021, from https://www.ted.com/talks/graham_allison_is_war_between_china_and_the_us_inevitable

26 Thucydides, Crawley, R., & Feetham, R. (1903). *Thucydides' Peloponnesian war*. London, UK: J.M. Dent and.

27 Allison, G. T. (2018, September). Is war between China and the US inevitable? Retrieved January 15, 2021, from https://www.ted.com/talks/graham_allison_is_war_between_china_and_the_us_inevitable

28 Allison, G. T. (2018, September). Is war between China and the US inevitable? Retrieved January 15, 2021, from https://www.ted.com/talks/graham_allison_is_war_between_china_and_the_us_inevitable

29 *Thucydides - Another Father of History? - The Peloponnesian War, Thucydides' Trap & Pericles Speech* [Video file]. (2019, January 20). Retrieved January 15, 2021, from https://www.youtube.com/watch?v=hYJyApvxr7U&ab_channel=SandRhomanHistory

30 Allison, G. T. (2018, September). Is war between China and the US inevitable? Retrieved January 15, 2021, from https://www.ted.com/talks/graham_allison_is_war_between_china_and_the_us_inevitable

[31] Allison, G. T. (2018, September). Is war between China and the US inevitable? Retrieved January 15, 2021, from https://www.ted.com/talks/graham_allison_is_war_between_china_and_the_us_inevitable

[32] *Thucydides - Another Father of History? - The Peloponnesian War, Thucydides' Trap & Pericles Speech* [Video file]. (2019, January 20). Retrieved January 15, 2021, from https://www.youtube.com/watch?v=hYJyApvxr7U&ab_channel=SandRhomanHistory

[33] Green, H. (Director). (2016, September 30). *Game Theory: The Science of Decision-Making* [Video file]. Retrieved January 21, 2021, from https://www.youtube.com/watch?v=MHS-htjGgSY&ab_channel=SciShow

[34] Smith, A. (1902). *The wealth of nations* (p. 160). New York: American Home Library

[35] Sonnenschein, H. F. (Director). (2015, December 1). *Game Theory and Negotiation* [Video file]. Retrieved January 21, 2021, from https://www.youtube.com/watch?v=E1ifAXKDyoI&t=580s&ab_channel=BeckerFriedmanInstituteatUChicago-BFI

[36] Engelhardt, L. M. (Director). (2016, August 9). *Game Theory* [Video file]. Retrieved January 21, 2021, from https://www.youtube.com/watch?v=Ldn34TxmGKE&t=1637s&ab_channel=misesmedia

[37] Chen, J. (2020, August 28). Nash Equilibrium. Retrieved January 22, 2021, from https://www.investopedia.com/terms/n/nash-equilibrium.asp#:~:text=The%20prisoner's%20dilemma%20is%20a,of%20communicating%20with%20the%20other.&text=The%20Nash%20equilibrium%20in%20this,players%20to%20betray%20each%20other.

[38] Currie-Knight, K. (219, December 17). Finite and Infinite Games (Carse) Explained. Retrieved January 23, 2021,

from https://www.youtube.com/watch?v=pODt-jnJfRA&t=14s&ab_channel=KevinCurrie-Knight

[39] Currie-Knight, K. (219, December 17). Finite and Infinite Games (Carse) Explained. Retrieved January 23, 2021, from https://www.youtube.com/watch?v=pODt-jnJfRA&t=14s&ab_channel=KevinCurrie-Knight

[40] Sinek, S. (Director). (2016, November 8). *What game theory teaches us about war* [Video file]. Retrieved January 25, 2021, from https://www.youtube.com/watch?v=0bFs6ZiynSU&ab_channel=TEDArchive

[41] Matthews, Dylan. "This Is the Best Letter of Recommendation Ever." Vox. Vox, June 6, 2015. https://www.vox.com/2015/6/6/8738229/john-nash-recommendation-letter

[42] Nash, John F. "Non-Cooperative Games." Dissertation, 1950

[43] Matthews, Dylan. "This Is the Best Letter of Recommendation Ever." Vox. Vox, June 6, 2015. https://www.vox.com/2015/6/6/8738229/john-nash-recommendation-letter

[44] Nasar, Sylvia. *A Beautiful Mind*. London: Faber & Faber, 2012

[45] Howard, Ron. 2001. A **Beautiful Mind**. United States: Universal Pictures.

[46] Porter, M. E. (2004). *Competitive strategy*. New York, NY: Free

[47] Porter, Michael E. "What Is Strategy?" Harvard Business Review, November 7, 2019.

[48] Byrne, John A. "How to Calculate the Cost of a Harvard MBA." Poets&Quants. MBA Watch, August 11, 2017. https://poetsandquants.com/2017/08/11/what-a-harvard-mba-now-costs/?pq-ab-2=b

[49] Porter, Michael E. "How Competitive Forces Shape Strategy." Harvard Business Review, May 20, 2015.

https://hbr.org/1979/03/how-competitive-forces-shape-strategy

[50] Porter, Michael E. "How Competitive Forces Shape Strategy." Harvard Business Review, May 20, 2015. https://hbr.org/1979/03/how-competitive-forces-shape-strategy

[51] Porter, Michael E. "How Competitive Forces Shape Strategy." Harvard Business Review, May 20, 2015. https://hbr.org/1979/03/how-competitive-forces-shape-strategy

[52] Porter, Michael E. "How Competitive Forces Shape Strategy." Harvard Business Review, May 20, 2015. https://hbr.org/1979/03/how-competitive-forces-shape-strategy

[53] Goldstein, David. "Who Moves The Coffee Markets? Meet The World's Largest Green Coffee Traders." Commodity Trading Guru, January 21, 2021. https://commoditytrading.guru/commodities/who-moves-the-coffee-markets-meet-the-worlds-largest-green-coffee-traders/.

[54] Barney, Jay. "Firm Resources and Sustained Competitive Advantage." *Journal of Management* 17, no. 1 (1991): 99–120. https://doi.org/10.1177/014920639101700108

[55] "Top 5 Highest Paid Footballer in Real Madrid." Great In Sports. G&S, September 12, 2019. https://greatinsports.com/top5/top-5-highest-paid-footballer-in-real-madrid/

[56] "Top 10 Highest Paid Stars In Kenya Premier League." Youth Village Kenya. Accessed February 7, 2021. https://youthvillage.co.ke/top-10-highest-paid-stars-in-kenya-premier-league/

[57] Porter, Michael E. "What Is Strategy?" Harvard Business Review, November 7, 2019. https://hbr.org/1996/11/what-is-strategy

[58] *BCG Matrix (Growth-Share Matrix) EXPLAINED.* Business To You, 2020.

https://www.youtube.com/watch?v=gNR49lk5dS0&ab
_channel=BusinessToYou

[59] *BCG Matrix (Growth-Share Matrix) EXPLAINED.* Business To You, 2020.
https://www.youtube.com/watch?v=gNR49lk5dS0&ab
_channel=BusinessToYou

[60] Hunger, J. David, and Thomas L. Wheelen. *Essentials of Strategic Management.* Essex: Pearson, 2014

[61] Hunger, J. David, and Thomas L. Wheelen. *Essentials of Strategic Management.* Essex: Pearson, 2014

[62] Banker, The. "The Banker's Top 100 African Banks 2020." The Banker - Unrivalled coverage of global finance & banking -, 2020.
https://www.thebanker.com/Banker-Data/Banker-Rankings/The-Banker-s-Top-100-African-Banks-2020?ct=true.
"Equity Ranks Position 7 in the List of Top 10 Banks in Africa in The Banker's Top 100 African Banks 2020." Equity Group Holdings, 2020.
https://equitygroupholdings.com/equity-ranks-position-7-in-the-list-of-top-10-banks-in-africa-in-the-bankers-top-100-african-banks-2020/

[63] Nelson, Erin. "Best Mission Statements: 12 Examples You Need to See." Fond, February 13, 2020.
https://www.fond.co/blog/best-mission-statements/

[64] "How to Write Your Mission Statement." Entrepreneur, October 30, 2003.
https://www.entrepreneur.com/article/65230

[65] Entrepreneur Staff. "Mission Statement Definition - Entrepreneur Small Business Encyclopedia." Entrepreneur. Accessed February 5, 2021.
https://www.entrepreneur.com/encyclopedia/mission-statement

[66] Miller-Wilson, Kate. "Best Examples of Strong Company Vision Statements." Example Articles & Resources. Accessed February 3, 2021.

https://examples.yourdictionary.com/best-examples-of-a-vision-statement.html

[67] Microsoft. "Our Corporate Values." About People. Accessed February 5, 2021. https://www.microsoft.com/en-us/about/corporate-values

[68] Publication. *Equity Group Holdings Plc and Subsidiaries Integrated Report & Financial Statements 2018.* Nairobi, Kenya: Equity Holdings Group PLC, 2019

[69] Adopted from Hunger, J. D., & Wheelen, T. L. (2014). *Essentials of strategic management* (4th ed.). Upper Saddle River, NJ: Pearson

[70] Bradfield, Ron, George Wright, George Burt, George Cairns, and Kees Van Der Heijden. "The Origins and Evolution of Scenario Techniques in Long Range Business Planning." *Futures* 37, no. 8 (2005): 795–812. https://doi.org/10.1016/j.futures.2005.01.003

[71] Peterson, G.D., Cumming, G.S. & Carpenter, SR (2003). Scenario planning: a tool for conservation in an uncertain world. *Conservation Biology*, 17 (2), 358-366. Retrieved from http://www.cakex.org/virtual-library/3420

[72] Bradfield, R., Wright, G, Burt, G., Cairns, G, & Van der Heijen, K. (2005). The origins and evolution of scenario techniques in long range business planning. *Futures*, 37,795-812. doi:10.1016/j.futures.2005.01.003

[73] Schoemaker, Paul J. "Forecasting and Scenario Planning: The Challenges of Uncertainty and Complexity." *Blackwell Handbook of Judgment and Decision Making*, 2004, 274–96. https://doi.org/10.1002/9780470752937.ch14

[74] Stauffer, D. (2002). Five reasons why you still need scenario planning. *Harvard Management Update*, Article Reprint No. U0206A, 3-5. Retrieved from http://hbr.org/product/five-reasons-why-you-still-need-scenario-planning/an/U0206A-PDF-ENG

[75] Coonradt, John E. "The Visionary and the Reactionary." Mackinac Center for Public Policy, March 24, 2005. https://www.mackinac.org/7012

[76] Schoemaker, Paul J.H. "Scenario Planning: a Tool for Strategic Thinking." *Long Range Planning* 28, no. 3 (1995): 117. https://doi.org/10.1016/0024-6301(95)91604-0

[77] Schoemaker, P J.H. "Scenario Planning: A Tool for Strategic Thinking Paul J. H. Schoemaker, Sloan Management Review (Winter 1995), Pp. 25–40." *Journal of Product Innovation Management* 12, no. 4 (1995): 355–56. https://doi.org/10.1016/0737-6782(95)97416-s

[78] Geldenhuys, C A. A change navigation-based scenario planning process: an afrocentric, developing country perspective., September 1, 2006. https://ujcontent.uj.ac.za/vital/access/manager/Repository/uj:8547

[79] Schoemaker, P J.H. "Scenario Planning: A Tool for Strategic Thinking Paul J. H. Schoemaker, Sloan Management Review (Winter 1995), Pp. 25–40." *Journal of Product Innovation Management* 12, no. 4 (1995): 355–56. https://doi.org/10.1016/0737-6782(95)97416-s

[80] Wulf, T., Meissner, P & Stubner, S. (2010). *A scenario-based approach to strategic planning – Integrating planning and process perspective of strategy.* (Working Paper 1/2010, HHL – Leipzig Graduate School of Management, Center for Scenario Planning – Roland Berger Research Unit, Leipzig, Germany)

[81] Schwartz, P. (2011, November 8th). Getting ahead of the curve. *Global Business Network.* Retrieved from http://www.gbn.com/ideas/scenarios.php

[82] Bradfield, Ron, George Wright, George Burt, George Cairns, and Kees Van Der Heijden. "The Origins and Evolution of Scenario Techniques in Long Range

Business Planning." *Futures* 37, no. 8 (2005): 795–812. https://doi.org/10.1016/j.futures.2005.01.003

[83] Turner, N. (2008). Future-proofing your organization. *CEO Journal*, 1–3. Retrieved from http://www.gbn.com/articles/pdfs/GBN_Futureproofing.CEO%20j.pdf

[84] Arriaga, Alexander F., David L. Hepner, and Angela M. Bader. "'However Beautiful the Strategy, You Should Occasionally Look at the Results.'" *Anesthesia & Analgesia* 126, no. 1 (2018): 16–18. https://doi.org/10.1213/ane.0000000000002492

BOOKS BY JOHN MUCAI

Shamba Shenanigans: A Collection of Riveting True Stories

A collection of riveting true-life experiences. Some stories are hilarious; others are thought-provoking, and others are likely to evoke different emotions as the story unfolds. Each story has one or more helpful life lessons.

The Endless Search for More: A Collection of True Stories on Money Matters

A collection of true stories that revolve around our continuous search for "more." And while this trait is essential for the long-term sustainability of humanity, John Mucai suggests that we must always strive to calibrate our desires appropriately. More importantly, we should adopt a problem-solving mindset in our never-ending quest for "more."

John Mucai

Historical Snapshots of The Great: What Can We Learn from Them?

The quality of life we enjoy today is a function of the many commendable actions taken by individuals in different spheres of life. Some of these people came before us many years ago, while others live among us. This book explores the lives of some significant historical figures to determine whether they share any common attributes we can emulate.

Seeking the Right Path: A Search for Spiritual Enlightenment

This book chronicles a personal search for spiritual enlightenment. John Mucai starts by finding out what religion means. He then examines the different religions and zeros in on five major ones: Christianity, Islam, Hinduism, and Buddhism. These religions have a combined following, comprising about 80% of the world's population. He examines their beliefs, practices, and sacred texts.

Most importantly, many complex questions emerge from the texts. While the book would be of immense interest to theologians, it is not a book on theology. Instead, it is an attempt by the author to seek spiritual enlightenment by sifting through the religious literature freely available to any ordinary citizen of the world.

The author's findings illuminate and hopefully give believers and non-believers a new perspective on religion.

Multiple Dilemmas: A Fictional Story of Multiple Ethical Dilemmas Based on True Historical Events

Multiple Dilemmas is a thriller based on historical events that raise significant ethical questions. The book delves deeply into challenging situations where ethical considerations are paramount, but the right choices are not clearly evident. The twists and turns in the story will keep the reader entranced for several hours.

Ngurario: A Traditional Kikuyu Marriage Experience

Ngurario is a true story of the multiple steps that John and Susan went through to formalize their marriage according to Kikuyu traditions. The book delves deeply into the drama, excitement, and joy they experienced along the way, right up to the final step in the journey, namely, an elaborate and colorful ceremony called *ngurario*.

Reminiscing on Basics: Fascinating Science and Maths Ideas for Everyone

Some ideas in science and math are so fascinating that it is a shame they are inaccessible to many people. This book attempts to fill the gap. Perhaps the curiosity triggered by these ideas will set a new intellectual journey into motion for some people, as it has done for the author.

One Day in the Year 3000

Nobody knows what the future holds one thousand years from now. But one can make some wild guesses. This book peeks into that distant future.

Archetypes of Human Existence: A New Perspective

No two of the more than seven billion people inhabiting the earth are the same. Even tweens have differences. Nature has bestowed on every individual unique attributes. And yet, the behavior of human beings can be reduced to a few archetypes. At the heart of the matter, each human being is one single entity comprised of a mind and a physical body, a mind that yearns for happiness and a body that longs for sustenance. And it is the interplay of these two needs that creates the different archetypes of humans.

This book explores a few of the archetypes. It discusses how the ideas around archetypes converge to offer a new perspective on fundamental questions that existentialists have grappled with for ages. The people described in the second chapter of this book are entirely fictitious. Any resemblance of their names to real people is purely coincidental. However, the characters are real and live among us. You may recognize some of them in your local community, your network of friends, or even in other human networks to which you are directly or indirectly connected.

Number One: Nothing Else Seems to Count

In the modern, highly competitive world, doing well in any competition is not enough. Being number one is what counts. This book traces the lives of five colorful individuals. They are winners in their unique ways from the early stages of their lives. We intimately experience twists and turns as they enter early adulthood and get embroiled in a contest anchored in the pursuit of business success and love. At some point, each character will realize that things can become highly complex, emotionally draining, and even dangerous when love is in the mix. The outcome of their respective pursuits to be "number one" is astounding. Indeed, the way the story ends offers readers tremendous food for thought.

John Mucai

Fun and Grit: Encounters of Farming Hobbyists

The stories in this book are primarily about people-the people of the shamba (small farm). After working for one of the biggest multinational companies and dabbling in a small-scale farming hobby, one of my insights is that every pleasant or unpleasant experience gives life its flavor.

Indeed, some of the unpleasant experiences add more spice to life. Having a nice laugh about something is the magic trick in many cases. Laughter is undoubtedly the best medicine for the soul.

INDEX